CIVIL DEFENSE IN THE SOVIET UNION

RAE

CIVIL DEFENSE IN THE SOVIET UNION

By Leon Gouré

GREENWOOD PRESS, PUBLISHERS
WESTPORT, CONNECTICUT

Library of Congress Cataloging-in-Publication Data

Gouré, Leon.
Civil defense in the Soviet Union.

Reprint. Originally published: Berkeley : University of California Press, 1962.
Bibliography: p.
Includes index.
1. Soviet Union--Civil defense. I. Title.
UA929.S38G68 1986 363.3'5'0904 86-337
ISBN 0-313-25162-2 (lib. bdg. : alk. paper)

Reprinted in 1986 by Greenwood Press, Inc.
88 Post Road West, Westport, Connecticut 06881

Printed in the United States of America

10 9 8 7 6 5 4 3 2 1

Foreword

Leon Gouré's *Civil Defense in the Soviet Union* leaves little doubt that the Soviet leaders are serious about civil defense and that the Soviet Union has an adequate civil defense organization. He states: "It is not a crash program, but one that seeks progressively to improve Soviet civil defense within the limits of a *relatively modest* annual expenditure of perhaps somewhere between 500 million and 1.5 billion dollars" [italics mine]. The important question is whether Mr. Gouré can establish his thesis and furnish conclusive evidence for it, since we, of course, have no such civil defense program in this country and since the relative strengths of the Soviet Union and the United States depend in no small degree on the relative civil defense positions. "Fortunately, however, in view of the large public participation in the civil defense program, the Soviet authorities cannot avoid revealing a certain amount of information on its implementation." Mr. Gouré pieces together this evidence in very considerable detail and in a most convincing way. He concludes that it is extremely likely that the Soviet Union has a civil defense much stronger than ours.

It is clear that the commandeering of labor and the construction of community or block fallout shelters is more practicable under the Soviet system than under our own. All they have to do is order it. We, of course, cannot do this and as a consequence we have to build single family shelters, which are much more expensive and much less efficient. "Civil defense in the USSR, known by the initials MPVO, is conceived on the principle that individuals, groups, communities, and important installations must be given some degree of protection against all types of weapons: conventional, chemical, bacteriological, and nuclear." Thus we see that the Soviet civil defense is aimed not only at nuclear fire power but at all likely war threats.

It is a pleasure to recommend *Civil Defense in the Soviet Union* to anyone concerned with this vital problem. It is too bad this book was not published earlier.

W. F. Libby

Department of Chemistry
University of California, Los Angeles

Preface

Any civil defense program is inevitably based on assumptions about the probability and the likely character of a future war, about the ways in which it might be initiated and conducted, and about the contribution that civil defense can make, among other things, to the country's defense and deterrence posture and to its recovery from an attack. Under the conditions of contemporary warfare no civil defense system could provide reliable protection for all citizens under all conceivable circumstances. Furthermore, both budgetary and technical limitations would probably rule out any attempt to design a system able to deal effectively with every threat and situation. On the other hand, a civil defense program has to be adequate for at least certain situations, the likelihood of whose occurrence must be rated high enough to justify a large investment of money and effort.

The Soviet approach to civil defense is no exception to this rule. Much of the interest it holds for us, therefore, lies in the light it casts on Soviet views about the international conflict and the nature of possible future wars. The main purpose of this study is to inquire into the doctrine of Soviet civil defense and describe the actual program that is being carried out, as well as to relate both doctrine and program to the more general attitudes and beliefs they reflect. The material and the discussion may also permit some insight into likely Soviet reactions should Western nations launch any large-scale civil defense programs of their own. The other Communist countries have not been touched on; although their programs, too, are of interest, this analysis is limited to the civil defense system of the Soviet Union, since most of the European satellite countries have patterned their activities on the Soviet model.

The first step toward any meaningful study of Soviet thinking on the subject is to ascertain the extent of actual activities and investments in civil defense. This is by no means easy to do. An analysis of civil defense manuals and instructions alone could be misleading; although they indicate doctrinal concepts and optimal goals, they do not provide a measure of the actual implementation of the program. Unfortunately, as is their policy in so many areas of Soviet life, the authorities maintain considerable secrecy about the civil defense effort, and have successfully withheld information pointing to the actual scope and preparedness of the organization. Thus, nothing has been published on the civil defense budget, the total numbers of persons engaged in civil defense organizations and those in training, the rate of shelter construction, the quantity and capacity of the various kinds of shelters already in existence, the size of stockpiles, or the availability of essential equipment. Even the whereabouts of existing shelters are veiled in secrecy, since under normal conditions no signs are posted showing their location.

Fortunately, however, in view of the large public participation in the civil defense program, the Soviet authorities cannot avoid revealing a certain amount of information on its implementation. In addition to numerous manuals, which are distributed in the Soviet Union in vast numbers, there are available the published speeches of military and civil defense officials, as well as a large amount of fragmentary information on local civil defense activities. These fragments are mainly reports, descriptions, or criticisms of local civil defense efforts, which are published in Soviet newspapers and magazines—a favorite Soviet method of advertising successful activities or publicizing failures as an example to others or to correct shortcomings. The articles cover a wide range of subjects, discussing such topics as the quality and progress of the training of civil defense units and of civilians, the numbers of instructors, the availability of equipment, the existence of shelters, training exercises, and popular attitudes.

The available information gains much in significance when it is viewed in the context of the Soviet Union's political and administrative systems and decision-making processes. Thus, the enactment of a civil defense program requires no public or legislative debate, but merely a decision of the leadership that is binding on all subordinate administrative, economic, and civil organizations. Moreover, the totalitarian character of the regime, and its system of centralized economic planning and resource allocation, enable the authorities to enforce and control the implementation of any program they favor. The Soviet leadership rarely launches mere paper programs, but tends to push vigorously for the execution of the programs it has decided to put through. This has been especially true of the civil defense program, which the authorities continue to publicize from year to year, in which they are investing relatively scarce resources, and which now calls for the compulsory participation of a majority of the citizens. Viewed in this context, the available information, though fragmentary, makes it possible to formulate conclusions of which one can be reasonably confident.

The purpose of this book is solely to acquaint the reader with civil defense activities in the Soviet Union and with some of the attitudes and views behind them. No comparisons, therefore, have been made between the Soviet system and similar Western programs. Nor is it my intention to argue for or against such a program for the United States. Rather, in line with the familiar argument that the more we know about the Soviet

Union the better equipped we will be to understand the motivations and intentions of its leaders, I hope to have cast some light on a relatively little-known and possibly important area of Soviet life and thought.

* * *

I am indebted to several colleagues in The RAND Corporation—Herbert S. Dinerstein, Alexander L. George, Herman Kahn, and Amrom H. Katz—for their valuable comments and help; to Mrs. Sibylle Crane and Miss Anita Magnus for their editorial assistance; and to Mrs. T. F. Halverson and her staff for the preparation of the illustrations.

This book is based on work undertaken by The RAND Corporation as a part of its continuing program of research for the United States Air Force.

LEON GOURÉ

November, 1961
Santa Monica, California

Contents

Illustrations

FIGURES

1

Background and Concepts

The threat of war has been a perennial preoccupation of Soviet leaders. In the official view that prevailed for almost forty years, communism and capitalism were engaged in a mortal struggle. The Communists' successful seizure of power in Russia had created an intolerable threat to the capitalist world, which consequently had to seek the destruction of its enemy, while the Soviet Union, in its turn, was committed to expanding the area under Communist rule. The unrelenting struggle between the two systems was expected to involve all possible means, including war. Lenin stated this view most clearly in 1919 when he said:

> We live not merely in a state but in a system of states and the existence of the Soviet Republic side by side with imperialist states for a long time is unthinkable. One or the other must triumph in the end. And before that end supervenes, a series of frightful collisions between the Soviet Republic and the bourgeois states will be inevitable.[1]

The thesis of the "inevitability of war" between the USSR and the capitalist powers remained a basic part of Communist dogma until February, 1956, when Khrushchev declared that, with the emergence of a number of Communist states and because of the growing military might of the Soviet Union, war was no longer "fatalistically inevitable."[2] But Khrushchev also insisted that war, although not "inevitable," still remained possible: "We deny the fatal inevitability of war. But, of course, no one can say categorically that there will be no war."[3]

Because of the ever-present danger of war, Soviet leaders, past and present, have been convinced that the Soviet armed forces and the country as a whole must always be maintained in a state of preparedness for this eventuality. Civil defense forms an integral part of this state of readiness, and its importance has steadily increased as a result of the growing danger to civilian populations which has been created by new weapons and strategies. Although the scope of the Soviet civil defense effort has varied in accordance with the requirements and anxieties of the moment, there has been some degree of investment and activity in the field of civil defense throughout the forty-four years of the Soviet state's existence.

In their approach to the problem of civil defense, the Soviet leaders had to take into account the various weapons available to their enemies. Since they believed the stakes in a war would be the life or death of communism or capitalism, they did not expect either side to be constrained by moral considerations in bringing all possible weapons to bear, or to spare any type of desirable targets.

Soviet Civil Defense before 1954

The Soviet authorities initiated the first civil defense measures as early as 1920. In those days, they were concerned over the possibility that their enemies would attack Soviet cities not only with conventional but also with chemical weapons. Thus, an article in a Soviet magazine in 1923 stated:

> Today no one has any further doubt that our political enemy will use chemical weapons in addition to other means of waging war.... Since a strategic aim in a future war will be... destruction of the national

centers providing supplies for the . . . army, the air fleet will be used for the bombing of cities, factories, railroad centers, etc., with chemical bombs.[4]

Fear of the possible use of chemical weapons against civilian populations was then fairly widespread in Europe, and was reflected, in 1939, in the distribution of gas masks to civilians in most of the warring countries. In the Soviet Union, this emphasis on chemical weapons was apparent from the very names of the paramilitary organizations that were charged at first with the training of civil defense personnel and later with the training of the population as a whole. The Society of Friends of Chemical Defense and Chemical Industry (*Obshchestvo druzei khimicheskoi oborony i khimicheskoi promyshlennosti*), for example, was organized in Moscow in 1924. It was reorganized in 1927 and expanded into the Society for Assistance in Defense and to Aviation and Chemical Development of the USSR (*Obshchestvo sodeistviia oborony i aviatsionnomu i khimicheskomu stroitelstvu SSSR*)—usually known by the abbreviation *Osoaviakhim*—which functioned until 1948. During the 1920's the Soviet Union manufactured gas masks for its armed forces and for training the population, and some gas-proof shelters were built.[5]

After 1931, Soviet civil defense planning became increasingly concerned with protecting cities from air attack, and great stress was placed on the threat posed by incendiary weapons. The growing danger of war resulting from Hitler's accession to the leadership of Germany led the Soviet Union to build more shelters, to expand its civil defense organization, and in 1935 to launch the first nationwide civil defense training program for the adult population.[6] A possible total of 38 million persons, principally members of the *Osoaviakhim*, the Red Cross, and industrial workers, were given a 20-hour civil defense course, and on its completion were awarded the badge "Ready for Air and Chemical Defense, 1st Grade."[7]

The civil defense system evolved in 1931 set the basic pattern of a civil defense organization that has remained in force, with few modifications, until today. It provided for the organization and training of civil defense units in cities, factories, and large economic, administrative, or public institutions, and of voluntary "self-defense groups" in nonindustrial facilities such as schools, scientific and cultural institutes, and apartment houses. The urban civil defense units were organized largely on the basis of various municipal departments and services, and their duties included alerting the population, maintaining public order, enforcement of blackout regulations, fire-fighting, medical assistance to casualties, rescue work, repair of damage, decontamination, bomb disposal, and supervision of shelter construction. Factory units were organized on the basis of the various shops and services and were responsible for all civil defense operations within the factory. The "self-defense groups" were recruited from among nonworking persons in the apartment houses or from the employees of nonindustrial institutions, and were primarily responsible for fire-fighting, first aid, enforcing blackout regulations, maintaining order in the shelters, and assisting in rescue work. A national staff controlled the planning and general organization of civil defense. On the local or city level, the civil defense system was closely tied to the army and to the local military chiefs responsible for the *passive* defense of the armed forces.

The measures instituted in the 1930's called for better protection of people and cities against enemy attacks with high-explosive, incendiary, and chemical bombs. Even though the Soviet political and military leaders hoped that future wars would be waged on enemy territory, they recognized that many of the Soviet cities were likely to become targets for air attack. A Leningrad propagandist wrote in 1939: "Leningrad is located at the junction of two worlds. In case of an armed conflict it can be subjected to an air attack in the very first minutes of the war."[8] But, as happens with so many plans in the Soviet Union, the implementation of the civil defense program fell short of its objectives. A limited number of protective suits were added to the gas masks, some simple fire-fighting equipment was distributed, first-aid teams were organized, and some new shelters were built; yet the number of trained civil defense personnel on the eve of World War II was far from adequate to the acknowledged need. The unsatisfactory state of Soviet civil defense drew this comment from Marshal Voroshilov, then the People's Commissar (Minister) of Defense, in his report to the 18th Congress of the Communist Party on March 14, 1939:

> I shall not dwell on what is known as passive defense . . . although the question is one that deserves to be spoken about at length. I would only say that the position in this respect is not good, owing not so much to the fault of us (the military men), as to that of civilian workers. This matter must be taken up more energetically and without delay.[9]

The Soviet Union used the period between the outbreak of the war in Europe in September, 1939, and the German attack on Russia on June 22, 1941, to expand and improve its civil defense. It also sought to learn from the experiences of the belligerents, notably those of England, which suffered heavy German air attacks after mid-1940. Even so, the Soviet civil defense organization was not fully ready at the time of the German invasion of Russia. For example, Leningrad, the second-largest Soviet city, with a population exceeding 3 million, had only some 14,000 civil defense workers.[10] By the end of August, 1941, this number had been hurriedly expanded to an official total of 196,198 workers, many of whom were inadequately trained.[11] Moreover, the lessons of the British experience with incendiary bombs had not been fully assimilated; Soviet civil defense literature and propaganda were still teaching the dangerous procedure of pouring water on incendiary bombs, or of dropping the bombs into barrels of water, rather than the far safer method of smothering them with sand.[12]

The German attack on the Soviet Union, and with it the threat of large-scale air attacks, prompted the general mobilization of the population for civil defense, based on the Soviet concept of massive public participation and self-help. On July 2, 1941, civil defense training and participation in civil defense work was made compulsory for all men and women between the ages of sixteen and sixty.[13] A compulsory 28-hour training course was instituted, which was estimated to have been passed by 98.9 million persons; it was supplemented in 1943 by an additional 10-hour course. In all, according to Soviet sources, 137,170,000 persons, including a large proportion of women, received civil defense training in the course of the war, and some 5.5 million of these were called upon to engage in civil defense work under enemy fire.[14] The regular civil defense units and the numerous "self-defense groups" were supplemented by militarized fire-fighting, rescue, and repair battalions and regiments.[15] Even though most civil defense units had only simple tools at their disposal, their wartime performance was generally good. The Soviet Union also acquired considerable experience in carrying out large-scale evacuations of residents and machinery from major cities.[16]

In the immediate postwar period, Soviet interest in civil defense declined. "Self-defense groups" ceased to exist, and compulsory mass training of the population was discontinued. Nevertheless, some activity in civil defense persisted, and various practices and institutions that had been established in wartime were carried over into the postwar period. The general structure of the civil defense organization was retained with the maintenance of a Main Administration for Local Anti-Air (Civil) Defense in the Ministry for Internal Affairs (MVD) and of civil defense administrations at republic, regional, district, and city levels.[17] Some efforts were made by the civil defense staffs and services to review their World War II experiences and continue their training.[18] The rule instituted in 1941 whereby plans for new buildings and factories had to meet "the requirements of civil defense" remained in force, and civil defense authorities continued to be included among the agencies that had to approve such plans.[19] Thus, there appears to have been a certain amount of shelter construction in new buildings even in the immediate postwar years. Finally, some civil defense training also was continued, as would appear from the complaint of a Soviet writer in 1947: "Recently a certain slackening has been noted.... Many ... groups have discontinued their systematic training and have given up studying.... One frequently now hears discussions on the 'dullness' of civil defense training."[20]

In 1952, mandatory study circles were instituted in the primary units of DOSAAF,* the organization formed in 1951 as a successor to *Osoaviakhim*.† The following year, participation in a 20-hour civil defense course was made compulsory for the entire DOSAAF membership, estimated at that time at over 15 million.[21] Despite these activities, however, the civil defense program was operating on a very low key, especially in the field of training. Furthermore, until 1954, it suffered from an astonishing failure to appreciate the significance of nuclear weapons and their implications for war and civil defense.

Soviet Attitude on Civil Defense after 1954

Despite the explosion of atomic bombs over Hiroshima and Nagasaki in 1945 and the growing U.S. nuclear stockpile in the

* The abbreviation stands for "Dobrovolnoe obshchestvo sodeistviia armii, aviatsii i flotu" (Volunteer Society for Assistance to the Army, Air Force, and Navy).

† In 1948 *Osoaviakhim* had been divided into three societies: DOSARM, or Volunteer Society for Support to the Army; DOSFLOT, or Volunteer Society for Support to the Navy; and DOSAV, or Volunteer Society for Support to the Air Force. In 1951 these societies were amalgamated into the all-Union DOSAAF organization.

years following, Soviet civil defense manuals published before 1954 ignored these developments.[22] Even the 1952–53 training programs made no reference to atomic weapons.[23] The reason appears to have been Stalin's inability or unwillingness to acknowledge publicly the significance of the emergence of nuclear weapons. Full realization of their implications had to wait until Stalin's death in 1953, and the development of a Soviet nuclear capability.[24] After that, both Soviet military doctrine and civil defense underwent extensive reappraisal in the light of the new weapons and of the new threats they had created.

The first mention of atomic weapons in Soviet civil defense manuals appeared in mid-1954.[25] This was followed by the publication of large numbers of books and manuals dealing with atomic and thermonuclear weapons. Although danger from conventional and chemical weapons continued to play a part, increasing emphasis was placed on the need to protect the population against nuclear weapons. In 1956 the civil defense authorities added bacteriological weapons to the list of possible threats.[26] Since then, Soviet civil defense has been concerned with the entire range of modern weapons. In 1955 the Soviet authorities also initiated a new and extensive civil defense preparedness program. It is still in effect today and will be described in subsequent chapters.

The renewed Soviet concern with civil defense appears to have been motivated by a number of factors: the development of strategic weapons of mass destruction that might be employed against the Soviet population, the Soviet Union's increasing vulnerability as a result of growing industrialization and the urbanization of its population, the polarization of the global struggle into a Western and Soviet power bloc, the intensification of the cold war, and the contribution that civil defense can make to the over-all military posture of the Soviet Union.

Soviet political and military leaders have repeatedly expressed their belief that in a future war each side would aim its attacks at the homeland of the enemy. As Khrushchev put it in his speech before the Supreme Soviet of the USSR on January 14, 1960:

> War would begin in the heart of the warring countries; moreover, there would not be a single capital, not a single major industrial or administrative center, not a single strategic area that would not be subject to attack, not only during the first days, but during the first minutes of the war.[27]

Moreover, modern strategic weapons are regarded as particularly suitable for employment against cities and large targets. A well-known Soviet military theoretician and propagandist, Major General N. Talenskii, wrote in 1959: "It should be kept in mind that modern weapons, by their very nature, are designed primarily to strike industrial areas, administrative and political centers, and communication facilities."[28] A Soviet civil defense manual states that the enemy is likely to attack "first of all large industrial centers of the state. . . ."[29]

From public statements it would appear that the Soviet leaders expect the belligerents to concentrate their attacks not on population targets as such, but only on cities that are important from an industrial, administrative, or political point of view, or on major communication and transportation centers. Some Soviet spokesmen suggest that the attacker (who is always understood to be the United States) is likely to send a major portion of his striking force against enemy strategic forces and military installations. Colonel I. V. Kravtsov, for example, writing in the house organ of the Soviet Air Force in 1957, gave this version of the American strategic air doctrine:

> The paramount task of the [U.S.] air force at the beginning of the war is considered to be the struggle for air supremacy. For this reason the first blows are planned to be directed against air bases, airfields, missile launching bases, the production and storage centers of nuclear weapons, aircraft factories, and fuel storage areas. . . .

The targets next in importance are considered to be oil-producing areas, military-naval bases, communication centers, industrial enterprises.[80]

Then, however, Colonel Kravtsov added:

According to American military doctrine, one of the principal targets of the air attack will be the population of the enemy. In a future war, therefore, the imperialist aggressors intend to subject large cities and densely populated regions to atomic and hydrogen bombardment and to attacks with chemical and bacteriological weapons for the purpose of destroying masses of peaceful citizens.

It is not clear whether this last statement was merely a piece of anti-American propaganda, or whether it represented the actual Soviet view of U.S. strategic doctrine. However, it is worth noting that Colonel Kravtsov put indiscriminate population attacks third in the alleged U.S. order of targets.

In this connection, Khrushchev and other Soviet leaders have repeatedly boasted that the Soviet Union, because of the greater dispersal of its population and industry, is less vulnerable to attack than is the West. Khrushchev, for example, said in his speech of January 14, 1960:

Of course, in the event of a new world war all countries would ultimately suffer in one way or another. We, too, would endure great misfortunes, we would have many losses, but we would survive. Our territory is immense and the population is less concentrated in major industrial centers than in many other countries. The West would suffer incomparably more.[81]

However, the distinction between an attack on the Soviet population as such and one on the important centers is largely academic, since most large Soviet cities are also major industrial or administrative sites and centers of communication. Furthermore, Soviet statistics indicate that population and industry are far more concentrated, and thus more vulnerable to attack, than is claimed by Khrushchev. During the past forty years, the Soviet Union has become transformed from a largely agrarian into a highly urbanized and industrialized country. Thus, in 1913 Russia had a total population of 159.2 million, of which only 18 per cent resided in cities; by 1960, the country's population had grown to 212.3 million, of which 49 per cent, or 103.7 million, lived in urban centers.[32] About 70 per cent of the total population resides west of the Ural Mountains. Even though the Soviet Union has fewer large metropolitan areas than the United States (as of 1959, there were only four Russian cities with a population exceeding a million,[33] and twenty-four such cities in the United States[34]), the Soviet urban population is nevertheless fairly concentrated. The twenty-five largest cities account for more than 24 million persons, or about 22 per cent of all the urban residents, while the 155 largest cities contain half the total urban population.[35] Furthermore, these cities are the principal administrative, political, and communication centers of the country and they contribute a major share of the Soviet industrial output. Thus, even if an enemy were to direct its attack against selected targets rather than general population centers, it could not avoid endangering the lives of many millions of Soviet citizens.

The Soviet leaders contend that such a war might involve every kind of weapon, especially nuclear, chemical, and bacteriological weapons of mass destruction. Said Marshal Zhukov in 1956: "A future war, if it is unleashed, will be characterized by the massive use of air force, many types of missiles, and various means of mass destruction such as atomic, thermonuclear, chemical, and bacteriological weapons."[36] This view was echoed by Khrushchev, who warned that the "logic of war" required the employment of all available types of weapons.[37] The "logic" in this instance flows from the Soviet leaders' belief that in a war between the Communist and Western power blocs, with each side bent on destroying the political, social, and economic systems of the opponent, neither would be restrained by moral considerations from employing the so-called weapons of mass destruction.

Soviet spokesmen, including Khrushchev, have frequently acknowledged that nuclear weapons, especially if delivered by ballistic missiles, constitute the greatest threat of all; and yet their mention of chemical and bacteriological weapons among weapons of mass destruction likely to be used is not merely rhetorical. As will be shown, Soviet leaders seem to consider quite seriously the possibility that chemical and bacteriological weapons might be used in strategic attacks against Soviet cities. Their concern seems to rest on a number of factors. Regarding bacteriological weapons, for example, a prominent Soviet scientist has pointed out that

> The most probable target of bacteriological weapons would be the distant rear of the enemy, since otherwise there would be danger of contagion to the troops and territory of the aggressor who employed this means of mass annihilation. Thus, the principal victims of biological weapons would not be the combatants, but the civilian population in the distant rear.[38]

Chemical weapons are thought to be, along with nuclear weapons, especially suitable for use in a "surprise attack" and comparable in effectiveness to small or medium atomic weapons, whereas bacteriological weapons are compared only with small atomic weapons.[39] One of the Soviet writers who seems to believe in the possibility of massive attacks with highly effective chemical agents says:

> The possible use of chemical agents on a large scale and the effectiveness of chemical weapons in inflicting casualties demands the timely preparation and institution of whole series of antichemical defense measures in the armed forces, as well as in the rear among the civilian population.[40]

Although chemical and bacteriological weapons are thought to be less effective than large-yield nuclear weapons, some Soviet commentators believe their effectiveness is being increased. Major General Talenskii, for example, said in a widely publicized article: "Nuclear weapons are not the only means of mass destruction in a future war. Thus, advances in missile techniques may radically increase the military effectiveness of chemical and bacteriological weapons. . . ."[41] Another military theoretician, Major General G. I. Pokrovskii has mentioned the "constantly increasing" effectiveness and variety of chemical weapons.[42]

There is no attempt to explain why an enemy should want to use chemical or bacteriological in preference to the admittedly more effective nuclear weapons. Most statements do not go beyond the allegation that the United States is planning chemical or bacteriological warfare, although some military spokesmen seem to imply the bilateral use of such weapons. In any event, the concern is real enough to have prompted the Soviet authorities to institute various civil defense measures designed to protect people against the effects of chemical and bacteriological attack.

Soviet military leaders firmly believe in the importance of civil defense, not only because the population as well as the economy must be protected in the event of a war, but also because they are convinced that an effective civil defense system contributes to the over-all defense capability of a country and to its preparedness for surviving an attack.[43] A Soviet military theoretician, in an article on Soviet military science and doctrine, relates civil defense directly to the military objectives of a future war:

> The role of the rear [homeland] has grown enormously in present-day wars and continues to grow. If the rear acquired a decisive role already during the First, and especially during the Second World War, then to an even greater degree the course and outcome of a future war will depend on the rear—victory being impossible without a highly organized rear of the country which is morally strong and economically and technologically powerful. That is why, from the very beginning of a future war, both sides will aim at destroying the operations and paralyzing the rear of the opponent and, on the other hand, will try to organize effective anti-air, anti-airborne, anti-atomic, anti-chemical and anti-bacteriological protection and defense of the rear.[44]

The internationally known Soviet physicist P. Kapitsa has expressed this relationship in broader terms:

> In the struggle for the prevention of atomic war it is essential to take into account the possibility that there will be found a reliable defense against nuclear weapons. If this is achieved by a country with aggressive intentions, then, being itself protected against the direct effects of nuclear weapons, it can much more easily decide to launch an atomic war.[45]

Such a defense could include civil defense as well as active anti-air defense, and a country possessing such means would be in a position, according to Kapitsa, to "impose its will on others."

It is not surprising, therefore, that Soviet military leaders have publicly endorsed civil defense as one of the means of strengthening the Soviet defense capability. Marshal Zhukov, in the above-mentioned speech, acknowledged the existence of a "real threat from the air" and went on to say:

> The task of defending the country's home front has never been so urgent as it is under present circumstances. The security of the Soviet people demands further efforts to improve the organization of civil defense against air attacks and the proper training of the entire population along lines of civilian organizations.[46]

These views were echoed by such other leading Soviet military personalities as Marshals Budenny, Biriuzov, and Vasilevsky. Biriuzov, for example, wrote that civil defense helped to "strengthen the defense capacity of the country."[47] Vasilevsky mentioned the growing "significance" of anti-aircraft and civil defense.[48] In February, 1958, Marshal Konev, then First Deputy Minister of Defense, told the Fourth All-Union Congress of DOSAAF that the training of the entire population in civil defense was of "exceptionally great importance for strengthening the defense capability of our country."[49] And Major General Pokrovskii listed civil defense in second place among a number of factors that, he said, form "one system" in Soviet military science.[50] More recently, in his address to the Twenty-Second

Congress of the Communist Party, the present Minister of Defense, Marshal R. Ia. Malinovsky, said on October 24, 1961, that since any major war would be likely to involve the use of nuclear weapons and missiles, ". . . we are forced to prepare our armed forces, the country, and the *entire people* to fight the aggressor, mainly under conditions of a nuclear war" [italics mine].[51]

Although the Soviet leaders now express increasing confidence in the Soviet Union's ability to deter a general nuclear war, they are not prepared to rely completely on this deterrent power, as is indicated by their continuing interest in developing a considerable civil defense capability for the USSR. Their insistence on the need to protect the Soviet population against possible enemy attacks with nuclear, chemical, and bacteriological weapons, and the extent of their investment in civil defense measures are evidence that they are serious about the need for civil defense and do not regard it merely as a sop to the population or as an instrument for maintaining public morale or for fanning hatred of the West. Soviet manuals state the need for a civil defense program quite simply: "The possession of atomic, chemical, and bacteriological weapons in the hands of the imperialists, and the threat of their use, forces us actively to prepare for civil defense."[52]

2

Scope and Organization of Soviet Civil Defense

Civil defense in the USSR, known by the initials MPVO,* is conceived on the principle that individuals, groups, communities, and important installations must be given some degree of protection against all types of weapons: conventional, chemical, bacteriological, and nuclear. To this end, the current doctrine calls for the massive use of manpower. The Soviet Union's widespread civil defense organization is based largely on existing civil administrative, economic, and service agencies, and is supported by a trained citizenry. According to the latest official handbook:

> The Local Civil Defense (MPVO) is organized in cities and populated points over the entire territory of the USSR. MPVO is a system of measures carried out by all governmental agencies and instituted for the purpose of protecting the population against all present means of attack from the air.
>
> MPVO measures are prepared and carried out mainly in peacetime, in all state, public, and coöperative enterprises, as well as in towns,

* Mestnaia Protivovozdushnaia Oborona (literally, "Local Anti-Air Defense").

workers' settlements, and inhabited rural points. These measures must ensure the uninterrupted work of all enterprises and institutions under conditions of attack from the air and prevent or reduce possible casualties among the population.[1]

Civil defense is centrally planned and controlled, and participation is compulsory for all federal, republic, territorial, and county or city civil administrations, as indeed for most populated places, industrial enterprises, institutions, and other large installations. The passage and enforcement of compulsory measures present few problems in the Soviet Union, where governmental decisions do not require public approval, where the legislature never rejects any measures desired by the leadership, and where the forced enlistment of administrations, organizations, institutions, and the people themselves in a variety of programs has become a normal feature of everyday life.

The duties of the MPVO are many and varied. They include:

. . . universal and compulsory training of the entire population in measures of defense against present means of attack from the air; the timely warning of the population and of all major installations of danger of attack from the air; the carrying-out of measures for sheltering and dispersing [evacuation] the population; the institution of blackout in cities and inhabited points and in installations of the national economy; the carrying-out of engineering and technical, fire prevention, and antiepidemic measures; and fulfilling the most urgent work for overcoming the effects of an attack from the air.

The duties of the MPVO also include the organization and execution of rescue work and the provision of the most urgent medical assistance to casualties, especially in centers of mass destruction.[2]

The MPVO, which is the civil defense organization proper, includes all full-time, part-time, special, and volunteer civil defense units and personnel. There are also military formations that perform special civil defense tasks. In an emergency, the regular civil defense units will be supplemented by large numbers of ordinary citizens who have been trained by DOSAAF and can be instantly mobilized. The law of 1941 that made every Soviet citizen liable to civil defense service in time of war is still in force, and current civil defense doctrine emphatically states that large elements of the population may be mobilized to help in dealing with the effects of an attack. The MPVO, although an independent agency, is closely tied to the executive organs at all levels of governmental and economic administration, to the military, and to the Communist Party.

The National Organization

Until January, 1960, Soviet civil defense was controlled by the Main Administration for Civil Defense, which was one of the agencies under the Ministry for Internal Affairs of the USSR, and was headed by a First Deputy Minister for Internal Affairs.[3] On January 13, 1960, the Ministry for Internal Affairs of the USSR was abolished,[4] and the present affiliation of the national civil defense organization is not clear. It may have come under the control of the Committee on State Security (KGB). More probably, however, it is now under the Ministry of Defense of the USSR, an arrangement that would appear plausible in view of the past close relationship between the MPVO and the military in general and the Air Defense Command in particular. For example, even though the MPVO was a civilian agency before 1960, its state of readiness was repeatedly discussed at Party congresses by the ministers of defense.[5] Also, the post of First Deputy Minister for Internal Affairs in charge of civil defense was last held by a Lieutenant General of Aviation, Oleg V. Tolstikov.[6] Since the abolition of the Ministry for Internal Affairs, Tolstikov has been promoted to the rank of Colonel General of Aviation, and Soviet press reports have described his presentations of medals to sappers who had distinguished themselves in bomb-disposal work, which has usually been a function of the MPVO troops.[7] It is possible, therefore, that Tolstikov is still head of the national civil defense organization, in which event his elevation in rank may be indicative of the greater importance attached to civil defense. Another fact that would argue for the supposition that civil defense is now under the Ministry of Defense is that, both nationally and at the local levels, the organization is largely militarized, with many officers serving on its staffs.[8] Moreover, it operates under regulations very similar to those of the Soviet Armed Forces.[9] Finally, as will be seen, the Armed Forces themselves perform certain civil defense functions in time of war.

Under the former setup, there was not only the post of First Deputy Minister for Internal Affairs in charge of civil defense but also that of Chief of Civil Defense of the USSR—probably also held by Tolstikov and quite possibly still in existence. Most likely, the First Deputy Minister dealt with administrative, budgetary, and general policy questions, whereas command and operational planning were the responsibility of the Chief of Civil Defense of the USSR. Under the latter was the so-called National Civil Defense Staff, in charge of planning, research, and organizational as well as technical civil defense problems. Among other responsibilities, this staff, under a chief of its own, defined the standards for shelter design, and it probably assisted in developing civil defense requirements for city planning and supervised the establishment and operation of civil defense schools.[10]

The standards, plans, and organizational schemes of the national staff are implemented by the various national ministries (Food, Trade, Health, Transportation, Communication, Construction, and so forth), each within its sphere of responsibility, and by subordinate civil defense staffs at various administrative levels. These staffs, whose personnel are full-time civil defense workers, form the nucleus of the civil defense organization.

Organization below the National Level

Below the federal staff and ministries, civil defense is set up on the basis of the territorial-administrative organization of the

Soviet Union. At every step, there is a chief of civil defense who is also a member of the executive branch of the local administration, and who is assisted by a permanent civil defense staff. Thus, at the top level of the member of republics of the USSR, civil defense is probably headed by the republic's deputy minister for internal affairs. Next, at the region (*oblast*) level, the organization will be headed by the chief civil administrator, the chairman of the executive committee of the provincial Soviet (council) of workers' deputies.[11] Similarly, the district or county (*raion*) and the city organizations are likely to be headed by the chiefs of the local civil administration (in the city, for example, by the mayor).[12] In city boroughs, the borough chairman of the executive committee heads the civil defense organization. In industry and transportation, civil defense is under the direction of the administrative chief of the installation. This system is designed to ensure the implementation of civil defense measures in peacetime. In wartime, all civil defense operations come under the jurisdiction of the civil defense staffs, whose chiefs work in conjunction with the active air defense forces.[13]

Local Civil Defense

In peacetime, then, the chief function of the above staffs and administrations is to attend to the implementation of such basic civil defense measures as the construction of shelters. In the event of a war, however, they have at their disposal various services and units that will conduct the actual civil defense operations both before and after an attack. According to the official handbook:

> Soviet civil defense doctrine . . . provides for the organization of the necessary services in all cities and populated points throughout the USSR, and institutes the necessary measures in all economic and administrative installations, as well as in all populated centers.[14]

In the larger cities, the MPVO chief and his staff supervise the organization and training of the civil defense services. In major industrial or economic installations, the responsible ministries will share in this supervision. Smaller towns and villages have no MPVO staff of their own, and the responsibility for civil defense rest with the civil authorities, who are subject to directives issued at the national level by the Main Administration for Civil Defense.

The city MPVO chiefs and their staffs, in organizing civil defense services and formations, have at their command (1) the various "services" based on different muncipal departments; (2) industrial civil defense services and formations; (3) self-defense groups recruited from among the nonindustrial population and organized in apartment buildings, schools, institutions, and villages; (4) militarized or military units; and (5) special civil defense units outside the city for use in disaster areas.

1. The Services

The services of the MPVO are created by the Executive Committees of the Soviets of Workers' Deputies for the purpose of timely preparation of the city for civil defense and to ensure the ability to overcome the effects of an atomic attack or other means of mass destruction. These tasks are carried out by the services for warning and communication, public order and safety, medical aid, fire-fighting, transportation, technical repair, trade and food, veterinary aid, blackout, shelter and cover, decontamination of persons and clothing, and decontamination of terrain and buildings.[15]

The "services" constitute the major element of local civil defense. They must work out the detailed plans for, and see to the execution of, civil defense measures in their individual areas of competence, and they are responsible for the training of civil defense units and for their use in time of war.[16] Each service is composed of a variety of units and teams that perform different tasks and reflect the various specialized muncipal departments, facilities, and organizations under its jurisdiction (see fig. 1). The medical service, for example, has twenty-three such units.[17]

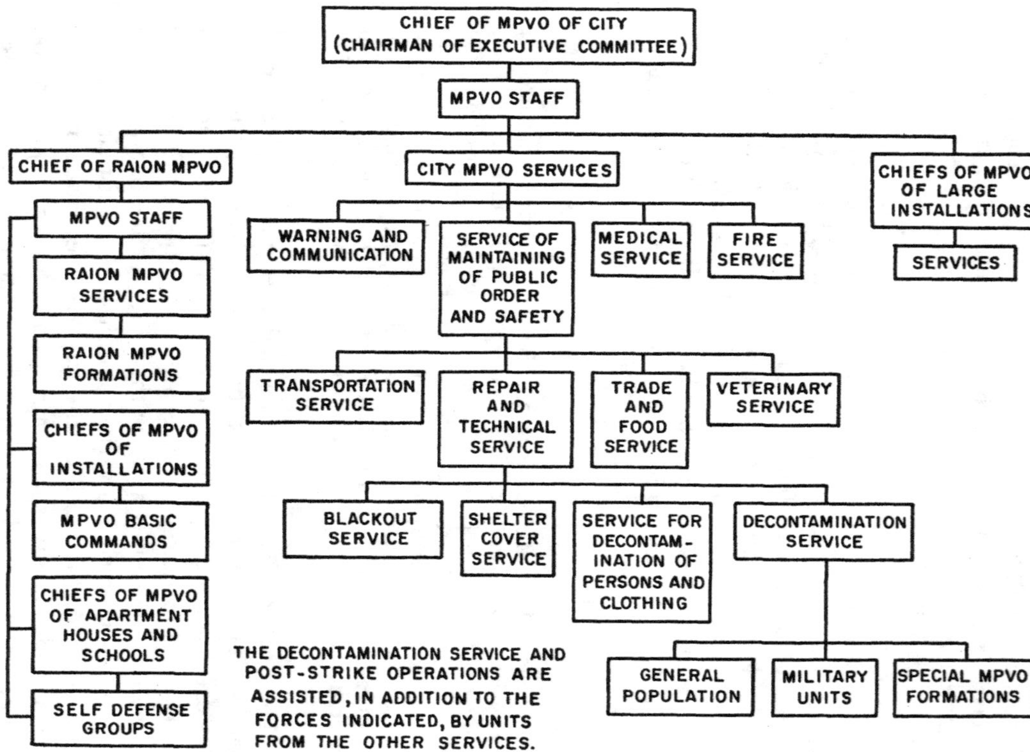

FIG. 1. Organization of civil defense services in a Soviet city or *raion* center.

WARNING AND COMMUNICATION SERVICE

Operating only in cities and in the district (*raion*) centers, this service is based on the telephone-telegraph, radio, and television services, which are controlled by federal and republic ministries. Its responsibilities include organizing the technical means of warning the population of danger, transmitting all civil defense signals to the people, and providing and operating communication facilities between the local operational civil defense staffs and their subordinate units.[18] During World War II, for example, all civil defense command centers and subordinate units in Moscow were provided with radio communication equipment in addition to the telephone and messenger services.[19]

SERVICE FOR MAINTAINING PUBLIC ORDER AND SAFETY

This service exists in the cities as well as in rural areas. Based on the police department, it informs the public of the various civil defense orders and warning signals, ensures that the citizens comply with the rules, and is responsible for preventing panic and controlling public behavior during alerts. Somewhat like air-raid wardens in World War II, its members must enforce public observance of civil defense regulations (including blackout rules), direct people to shelters or first-aid stations, guard industrial facilities and water and food supplies against sabotage, report on possible contamination by radiological, chemical, or bacteriological agents, enforce quarantine in contaminated areas, assist in evacuations, and report the effects of enemy attacks to the district civil defense staffs.[20]

MEDICAL SERVICE

This service, recruited from the public health department and other health and medical institutions, plans for and carries out all medical duties, including evacuation of the wounded, epidemic control measures, and the quarantining of areas suspected of having been under bacteriological attack. It organizes and trains various specialized units for medical first aid and for rescuing people from disaster areas, and it also plans and supervises the decontamination and medical processing of persons who have been exposed to nuclear, chemical, or bacteriological weapons. In some of its functions it is assisted by the Soviet Red Cross and Red Crescent, which organize units that will search for and remove the wounded. The Medical Service operates under the supervision of the Ministry of Public Health, rather than within the narrower frame of a city or district government, because of its need to make use of medical facilities that are outside the cities and thus beyond the jurisdiction of any local civil administration.[21]

TRANSPORT SERVICE

This service came into existence in 1958, when civil defense authorities became seriously interested in plans for evacuating civilians from the cities, and it is organized only in cities. It must provide transportation for city evacuation, for moving people out of disaster areas, and for bringing MPVO personnel and matériel into such areas. Working in coöperation with evacuation committees of the city boroughs, the transport service is responsible for drafting transportation plans involving all available means (railroads, river boats and ferries, air transport, and vehicles), and for determining the evacuation procedures. It is also responsible for the decontamination of its own equipment.[22]

REPAIR AND ENGINEERING SERVICE

This service is based on the Construction Administration and on various departments and institutions of the muncipal economy and utilities. It plans and institutes engineering and technical measures for the purpose of hardening vital public constructions and communal service networks, such as water, sewage, gas, and electricity. Moreover, it is responsible for organizing and training civil defense units, some for rescuing people who are trapped in buildings in the disaster area, and others for repairing vital installations and municipal services.[23]

TRADE AND FOOD SERVICE

For the purpose of supplying people from disaster areas with the necessary food and a minimum of other essential goods, the Trade and Food Service is organized in cities and district centers on the basis of the trade departments of the local soviets and other state organizations. Its task is greatly facilitated by virtue of the state-ownership of most trade storage and retail facilities and organizations and by the state's ability in time of war to requisition private supplies. Aside from its supply function, the service takes measures to protect food and other supplies from contamination by toxic or radioactive agents, and it is also responsible for the disinfection and decontamination of warehouses and supplies and for the reprocessing or destruction of contaminated food and fodder.[24]

FIRE-FIGHTING SERVICE

This service is based on the fire department, which until 1960, similarly to the national civil defense organization itself, was under the over-all control of a Main Administration of Fire Protection (one of the agencies of the Ministry for Internal Affairs of the USSR) and subordinate administrations in the regional or lower levels of government.[25] The Fire-Fighting Service is responsbile for devising fire-prevention measures, supervising their execution, training the personnel necessary to fight widespread conflagrations, and directing the work of all fire-fighting units after an attack.[26]

BLACKOUT SERVICE

Based on the electric power department, the Blackout Service plans and executes all measures necessary for a successful blackout, and provides electricity to important facilities and essential units in disaster areas.[27]

SHELTER AND COVER SERVICES

Based on the housing departments of the executive committees of the local soviets and of related municipal agencies, the Shelter and Cover Service checks on the condition and state of readiness of shelters and other kinds of cover and ensures that they are used correctly. Furthermore, it prepares maps of city blocks and buildings to facilitate the rapid location of shelters, and the evacuation of people from them in the event of large-scale destruction.[28]

SERVICE FOR THE DECONTAMINATION OF PERSONS AND CLOTHING

This service relies on the various public baths and laundry services, which in the Soviet Union are usually owned and operated by the municipal authorities. It organizes stationary or mobile facilities for decontaminating persons and clothing in or near the disaster areas, and stocks the supplies necessary to the performance of this task.[29]

SERVICE FOR THE DECONTAMINATION OF TERRAIN AND BUILDINGS

Being based on the street-cleaning, construction, engineering, and several other municipal departments, this service has a variety of functions. It organizes and equips reconnaissance units charged with determining not only the degree but the nature of contamination (whether radioactive, chemical, or bacteriological). It forms units that will do the actual decontamination work, makes plans for utilizing municipal facilities and equipment for this purpose, and stocks the necessary material and supplies. After an attack, the service will be supported by the rescue, fire-fighting, medical, and public order and safety services of the MPVO, by special civil defense units, and possibly by units of the armed forces. The local civil defense chiefs also are authorized to mobilize elements of the population in support of the Decontamination Service.[30] Independently of this service, the decontamination of the contents of buildings is the responsibility of the individual citizens.[31]

VETERINARY SERVICE

This service is organized only in rural areas, on the basis of agencies dealing with agriculture and animal husbandry. It controls all measures for the protection of livestock, water sources, and fodder, and trains the veterinary personnel whose task it will be to protect, treat, and evacuate livestock in the event of an attack.[32]

2. Civil Defense in Major Installations

For factories, railroad yards, shipyards and ports, dams, power plants, and the like, the civil defense organizations vary according to the size and importance of the installation itself. The less important are under the *raion* (district) civil defense staff, whereas the major ones answer directly to the city civil defense staff. The chief of the organization is invariably the administrative head of the installation, assisted by the chief engineer and other technical personnel and by the Party Secretary. Major installations may in addition have civil defense inspectors from the ministry or other high-level agency that has jurisdiction over the installation.

Large installations have "services" similar to those of a city, with each service recruiting its own civil defense unit from among the employees of departments or shops of the installation. Here, the main services are Warning and Communication, Public Order and Safety, Medical, Fire-Fighting, Repair and Engineering, Blackout, Antichemical and Radiation Defense, and Shelter and Cover.[33]

A typical large installation will have a great many people participating in the various civil defense services. Thus, the Warning and Communication Service consists of two units; the Public Order and Safety Service has from two to five squads of 14 persons each; the Medical Service may have several commands, depending on the number of persons employed by the installation (but not less than two commands of 316 persons each, according to the current Soviet handbook); the Fire-Fighting Service may have several units of 36 persons each, in addition to the installation's regular fire brigade; the Shelter Service will have a team of five for every 150 persons sheltered; and so forth.[34]

Smaller factories and installations organize all-purpose units (*unitarnye komandy*), staffed by employees who are trained in various special skills, and subdivided into teams and squads for such specific tasks as medical aid, fire-fighting, shelter services, and repairs.[35]

3. Self-Defense Groups

In keeping with the belief that civil defense is needed wherever people work or live, the current program has reinstituted the so-called "self-defense groups," which numerically formed the major part of the Soviet civil defense organization during World War II. Self-defense groups today are organized in non-industrial installations and institutions in the residential sections of towns, and in rural areas; that is, in administrative offices, research centers, public institutions, schools, museums, apartment houses, and farms. As in the other MPVO organizations discussed above, membership in self-defense groups is compulsory (although people may volunteer for it), and is recruited from among men between the ages of 16 and 60, and women between 18 and 50:

> It is known that self-defense groups (or all-purpose units) recruit on a compulsory basis persons not liable to obligatory military service, or

> who are deferred from the draft, from among citizens of both sexes: women between the ages of 18 to 50 and men between 16 and 60. In staffing self-defense groups (all-purpose units) it must be kept in mind that persons temporarily disabled as a consequence of illness or injury, invalids, pregnant women, and other citizens listed in the [decree on the] "Establishment of Self-Defense Groups of MPVO" are not to be included.[36]

A person may serve in two units simultaneously: one at his place of work and another at his residence.

In the cities, the number and location of self-defense groups is determined by the MPVO chiefs of the city or of the individual city boroughs; in rural areas the decision lies with the chief of the district *(raion)* MPVO. The number of self-defense groups will depend on the number of persons residing or employed in an installation, building, or area. In the cities it is usual to have one group for every 300 residents or employees in a building, though in very large buildings one group may serve as many as 500 persons or even more.[37] A single group may also serve a whole block or even an entire street if none of the buildings houses the required number of persons. In rural areas, one self-defense group is organized for every 500 or more persons. Villages with only 200 to 500 residents will have all-purpose (*unitarnoe*) units to handle all civil defense tasks.[38]

As in other civil defense organizations, every self-defense group is headed by the chief administrator of the establishment or area, and each administrative head has under him an operational chief who directs the training and work of the group.

The typical self-defense group is divided into various specialized teams. As shown in figure 2, these include a command team composed of the operational chief, a property officer, a communication man, and a political officer. There is also a six-man team for surveillance and maintenance of order, a seven-man fire-fighting team, a seven-man antichemical team, a six-man repair and rescue team, and an eight-man medical

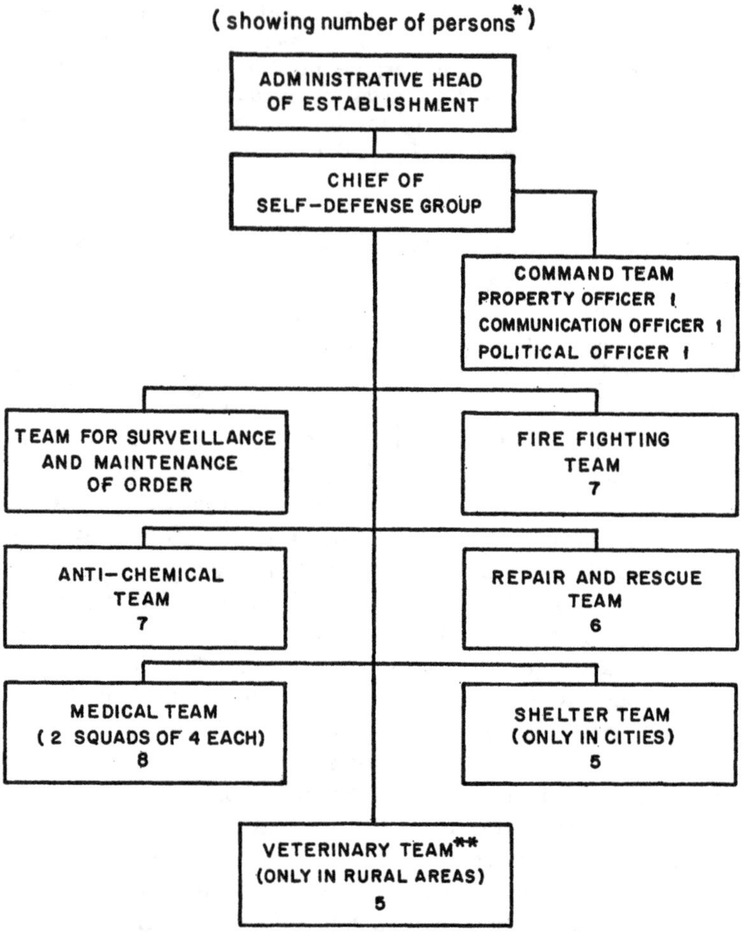

FIG. 2. Organization of a self-defense group.

* In addition to the regular members of the groups, whose numbers are given here, each team has two reserve members.

** In the veterinary team, one person is added for every fifty head of cattle exceeding a hundred.

team. In cities and worker settlements there will be, in addition, a five-man shelter team; in rural areas, a five-man veterinary team. Every team must also have two reserve members. The shelter team may be larger, since the rules call for five men for a shelter with a 150-person capacity, and for correspondingly larger teams for bigger shelters. The basic veterinary team is supposed to handle from 30 to 100 head of livestock, and will have an additional person for every 50 head of livestock above that number.[39]

The self-defense groups are trained by the local DOSAAF committees and the local Red Cross, with the assistance of, and according to programs devised by, the responsible civil defense staffs and the local civil defense schools that also train regular civil defense personnel.[40] In 1959 the training consisted of 25 hours of lectures (15 hours for the group as a whole and 10 for each team in its own specialty) and up to 10 hours of practical work and exercises.[41]

4. Special MPVO Formations

The organizational scheme of Soviet civil defense calls for special civil defense units in addition to those listed above. Some of these units are recruited from educational or medical services in the cities. For example, the MPVO staff can order students in the last two years of high school and the first three semesters in institutions of higher learning to be organized into casualty-search and stretcher-bearer units of 125 persons.[42] Most special MPVO formations, however, are intended to assist the cities in rescue, fire-fighting, repair, and decontamination work, and hence must be located outside the cities, where they run less danger of being destroyed by a nuclear attack, and from where they can not only aid nearby cities but also help the rural areas to deal with the effects of an attack.

> In each collective and state farm, independently of the existing self-defense groups, there are formed special commands for the purpose

of overcoming the effects of an attack on the threshing floors, in the fields, in the nearby forests, and in other agricultural areas. In collective and state farms and settlements located near large industrial and administrative centers, there are organized other formations for the purpose of coming to the assistance of cities that are subjected to atomic attack, such as, for example, reconnaissance groups, which reconnoiter the territory of their district or city.[43]

According to a civil defense handbook, the large collective farms are to organize special technical units of about 200 persons each, which will have heavy equipment for fire-fighting, decontamination, and rescue work.[44] The rural areas also organize larger units (of 400 persons each) to assist the regular city and rural civil defense organization in the disaster areas, and units of up to 500 persons for decontamination work in the countryside. These units are to be kept in a constant state of readiness.[45] Village youth, students, and rural medical personnel are to be organized into search and stretcher-bearer units and first-aid units.[46]

5. Military Units

During World War II, as noted earlier, large cities in the Soviet Union had some militarized MPVO battalions and regiments. Current civil defense manuals suggest that elements of the Soviet armed forces would again participate in civil defense operations in the event of a war. Such military units would be called upon to carry out radiological reconnaissance from helicopters and ground vehicles, deal with unexploded bombs, and perhaps participate in rescue and decontamination work.[47] We know little about the size and character of these forces, but there is evidence that they exist. In September, 1957, for example, an article in the newspaper *Red Star* mentioned a competition between "regiments and subordinate units of the MPVO troops of the country."[48]

Size of the MPVO

The Soviet Union has published no official data on the size of its civil defense organization. Apparently, a relatively small group of full-time personnel concentrates mainly on the central administration and the various staffs, whereas the main body of the organization consists of part-time participants who are either employees of muncipal services or industrial installations or members of self-defense groups. Since the organization of civil defense services and their subordinate units is compulsory for cities, districts, and economic installations, one may assume that they exist, and evidence from the Soviet press supports this conclusion.[49] There is also considerable evidence pointing to the existence of self-defense groups in cities and rural areas.[50]

Training, equipment, and the degree of readiness of these different units are likely to be uneven. In 1958, for example, a Soviet publication complained that the training and equipment of self-defense groups in apartment houses was often inadequate:

> Residential self-defense groups play an important role in the organization of civil defense. Nevertheless, district committees and primary organizations of DOSAAF are still paying little attention to the preparation of this side of the system. Practical training is not being carried out in such groups, and there is a shortage of the equipment prescribed under the regulations.[51]

Undoubtedly, self-defense groups in apartment houses have a lower priority than units in industrial enterprises or public institutions, since the Soviet civil defense system in general puts protective measures for administrative, industrial, and control institutions ahead of those for the general public. Soviet press reports, however, point to constant efforts to improve the training and equipment of all civil defense units, and there are fairly frequent mentions of training exercises for self-defense groups.[52]

All indications are that the MPVO disposes over a large and far-flung organization. Khrushchev is reported to have boasted:

> The USSR has at its disposal a well-organized corps of more than twenty-two million men and women who are all trained in civil defense. This represents 10 per cent of the total population of the Soviet Union. Each year an additional five million persons are trained in civil defense.[53]

Speculating on whether a force of this size is actually in existence or represents merely a goal, a Canadian intelligence officer noted in a recent article: "Working on the ratio of one team per approximately 500 population, however, the 22 million figure quoted would indicate that this has probably been achieved."[54]

Relationship to the Communist Party

Officially, Soviet civil defense at all levels is headed by and is responsible to the executive-administrative branch of the civil government. In practice, like other government agencies, it is subordinated to the Party, for the Party organization parallels and supervises the entire administrative-governmental system. Thus, the former Main Administration for Civil Defense was responsible to the Council of Ministers of the USSR and to the Central Committee of the Party. Similarly, the civil defense chiefs at lower levels—be they republic ministers or executive committee chairmen for a region, district, or city—answer to the corresponding Party committees. The Party supervises every section of the MPVO, from the civil defense staffs down to the self-defense groups; in the large organizations this supervision is exercised by Party committees, and in the smaller ones, by political officers.[55]

Although the highest Party leadership, with the exception of Marshals Voroshilov and Zhukov, has refrained from making public statements on civil defense, this is not true of the lesser Party officials. Members of the Central Committee of the Communist Party of the USSR and representatives of republic, regional (*oblast*), and city Party committees have attended DOSAAF congresses and made speeches in support of civil defense training.[56] Republic and regional Party bureaus, as well as city and subordinate Party committees, have issued resolutions to expand local DOSAAF groups and civil defense schools and have held joint meetings with corresponding DOSAAF committees.[57] For example, the Secretary of the Kostroma *oblast* Party Committee reported:

> In order to draw the attention of Party, soviet, trade union, and economic leaders to questions of mass defense work, following the decision of the *oblast* Party Committee Bureau, joint meetings were held this year in all cities and *raions* of the *oblast*. As a result of sharp and just criticism, many Party organizations improved the leadership of the DOSAAF groups.[58]

The Soviet press also mentions that local Party organizations have been guiding and supervising civil defense training in local DOSAAF organizations, and the secretaries of primary Party organizations are said to have been instructed to encourage, supervise, and participate in civil defense training.[59] Furthermore, both the MPVO and DOSAAF work in close coöperation with the Young Communist League (*Komsomol*), whose members help to organize civil defense units and participate in the training programs.[60]

Although most of the MPVO national leadership and staffs are military personnel, many of these are at the same time members of the Communist Party. Tolstikov, for example, the former (and possibly the present) national head of MPVO, was at one time a member of the Central Committee of the Azerbaijan Communist Party.[61] The chiefs of civil defense organizations of republics, regions, cities, and boroughs are not only the heads of the civil government but also Party members, and many of them are likely to have held Party posts at one time or another. In general, the organizational committee (*orgkomitet*) of the local

DOSAAF body tends to coöperate closely with the corresponding Party committee. *Orgkomitet* chairmen are nearly always Party members. They are nominated for the chairmanship by the responsible Party committee—one of the methods by which the Party maintains control and supervision over non-Party organizations.

The MPVO Budget

Neither the Soviet government nor the civil defense administration ever publishes any information on the Soviet civil defense budget, and thus it cannot be computed accurately. At both the national and local levels, expenditures are apportioned among many agencies, departments, and organizations whose budgets do not identify civil defense items and thus hide their costs. This applies not only to the funds necessary to operate, train, and equip the various civil defense services and units, but also to the cost of shelter construction, the hardening of various facilities, and the like.

Many of the expenditures are absorbed variously by municipal or *raion* budgets, the budgets of factories and economic ministries, the funds of DOSAAF, the Red Cross, and the military budget. Thus, the city governments pay for the equipment of the city's civil defense services and self-defense groups in residential buildings under the city's jurisdiction.[62] The cost of equipping and training civil defense units in factories or economic installations, and that of self-defense groups in apartment houses controlled by these installations, is borne either by the ministry or other organizations to which they are subordinated or by the installation itself.[63] Similarly, the financing of shelter construction rests largely on the organizations that will use the shelters in time of war.[64] Public shelters and those in apartment houses are paid for from the muncipal housing fund, while ministries or institutions pay for shelter construction in the factories, institutions, and apartment houses operated by them. On state and collective farms, the expenses of the self-defense groups and other civil defense measures are met by the farm budget.[65]

DOSAAF is largely self-suporting, deriving most of its income from membership dues. Some assistance comes from the armed forces, which, for example, publish some civil defense training manuals and handbooks. Material and financial aid to local training groups is also sometimes provided by trade-union organizations.[66] Thus, it is quite apparent that the Main Administration for Civil Defense bears only a part, and possibly a small part, of the total civil defense cost.

Although the exact Soviet civil defense budget is not known, estimates have been made of the Soviet Union's possible annual outlay for the various civil defense measures and equipment that will be described in the subsequent chapters. One such estimate was reported in the testimony given by Mr. Frank B. Ellis, Director of the Office of Civil and Defense Mobilization, to a subcommittee of the House Committee on Appropriations. According to Mr. Ellis, "a secret report . . . showed Russia was spending from $500,000,000 to $1,500,000,000 a year" on civil defense.[67] Even such a relatively modest expenditure, which is fully within the Soviet capability, would be a measure of the seriousness with which the Soviet leadership regards civil defense. Over the years, this expenditure has bought a substantial amount of protection for the population.

3

Training the Population

Soviet writers and official spokesmen cite a number of reasons for the importance of civil defense training: (1) A trained population will not suffer the degree of trauma and panic experienced by the people of Hiroshima and Nagasaki, who had no previous knowledge of atomic weapons. (2) Adequate training will prevent many casualties in the event of an attack. (3) A population trained in civil defense can practice self-help, and can, of course, be mobilized to help in repairing the damage and treating the casualties caused by an attack. (4) Civil defense training strengthens the defense capability of the Soviet Union.[1]

On the last point in particular, Soviet military leaders have been most emphatic. Thus, Marshal Biriuzov, now in command of Soviet Anti-Air Defense, wrote in 1956: "This noble task [civil defense training] is aimed directly at strengthening the defense capability of our country."[2] A year later, Marshal Malinovsky (the present Minister of Defense) praised DOSAAF for its "great role in strengthening the defense capability of our great country."[3] First Deputy Minister of Defense Marshal

Konev said to the Fourth All-Union Congress of DOSAAF in 1958:

Each Soviet citizen, each boy and girl, must always be ready to enter the ranks of the fighters of the MPVO. They must actively and persistently study the means of anti-air, anti-atomic, anti-chemical, and anti-bacteriological defense. This is a difficult but at the same time honorable task. It is of exceptionally great significance for strengthening the defense capability of our country.[4]

Marshal Vasilevsky and Lieutenant General S. Shatilov, the latter a deputy chairman of the Central Committee of DOSAAF, have expressed similar views.[5]

As noted earlier, the responsibility for civil defense training of the population and of the self-defense groups rests with DOSAAF, which is assisted by the Red Cross and Red Crescent societies and which coöperates closely with Party, Komsomol, and trade-union organizations.

DOSAAF—Its Functions and Organization

Like its predecessor, the *Osoaviakhim,* DOSAAF is a voluntary paramilitary mass organization, whose primary purpose is to teach skills and establish or perpetuate traditions that will be of value to the Soviet armed forces. Thus, it trains the population, especially the young people, in such skills as marksmanship, skiing, diving, parachute jumping, piloting of planes, radio operations, truck driving, and mechanics, and helps to develop general physical fitness by promoting various sports. DOSAAF members also study military history and lore, and familiarize themselves with weapons; they make scale models, learn how to train dogs, and study seamanship. Civil defense training is obligatory for all members, who appear to have received this training ahead of the general population. Administratively, DOSAAF is under the control of the Ministry of Defense,[6] but it also maintains close ties with the MPVO, the Komsomol, and the Ministry of Education.

The DOSAAF organization follows the territorial-administrative principle, with an All-Union Central Committee and Presidium (elected by an All-Union DOSAAF Congress) at the top, and committees at the republic, *oblast, raion,* city, and borough levels. At the bottom are the primary organizations, which operate study circles on a variety of subjects. Every DOSAAF member must belong to such a group, either at his place of work or in his neighborhood. It is here that he pays his membership dues, which are used to finance the primary as well as the higher organizations.[7] DOSAAF publishes its own national newspaper (*Soviet Patriot*) and several magazines. Some republic organizations have additional publications of their own.

DOSAAF is the largest voluntary society in the USSR. Since it does not publish any figures, its exact membership is not known. In 1952 it was estimated at 15 million. In view of the intense membership drive of the past ten years, and the admitted goal of recruiting the majority of all adults by 1962, DOSAAF is believed to have more than doubled its membership since 1952.[8] Some regions and districts claimed to have recruited 60 to 80 per cent of their adult population.[9] Another indicator of DOSAAF's size is the report that in 1959 "about two million persons" were elected to membership on DOSAAF committees.[10] DOSAAF's current aim is to "attract the majority of the adult population to become members of the society."[11]

DOSAAF's ties to the military establishment are reflected in the preponderance of military men in its All-Union Presidium and Central Committee and in its efforts, at lower levels, to recruit retired or reserve officers for committee work and as instructors.[12] The post of chairman of the Presidium was long held by Colonel General P. Belov and is now occupied by General of the Army D. D. Leliushenko, with Lieutenant General S. Shatilov as deputy chairman. The All-Union Central Committee of DOSAAF includes Marshal Budenny and Lieutenant General Tolstikov, head of the former Main Administration for Civil Defense. Also on the Central Committee are a First Deputy Chairman of the Presidium of the Red Cross and a member of the Bureau of the Komsomol Central Committee of the USSR—two large organizations that work closely with DOSAAF and many of whose members also belong to DOSAAF. The Komsomol alone has more than 18 million members.[13] The Red Cross and Red Crescent societies, with a combined membership of over 23 million, not only train their own members in medical first aid but also provide medical units for civil defense operations and supply instructors to teach first aid to DOSAAF members.[14]

Organization of the Training Program

The present intensive effort to train large elements of the population in civil defense was initiated only in 1955. Since then, DOSAAF has steadily expanded its program, which involves training its own members and those of self-defense groups, and generally organizing and supervising the compulsory training of the adult population. All men between the ages of 16 and 60 and women between 16 and 55 are liable to civil defense training if they are physically fit.[15] "People more than 16 years of age receive civil defense training in circles organized by DOSAAF primarv organizations at places of work, schools, residential buildings, and so forth, in coöperation with the managements of these enterprises."[16]

Once or twice a week, the trainees meet in small study groups of from ten to twenty-five, either after working hours or at times arranged with the administration of the installation or organization to which they belong.[17] Meeting space is provided either by the district committee or by the management of the factory, institution, school, or apartment house to which the primary organization belongs. Since the courses tend increasingly to emphasize practical work, much of today's training takes place in local civil defense schools or in special training installations established in residential areas or at places of work.[18]

FIG. 3. Civil defense training poster.

Instructors are provided and trained by DOSAAF; those for the first-aid classes are supplied by the Red Cross. A great many of them are retired or reserve military men and professional people. Supposedly, they are all volunteers. In truth, many instructors probably are "volunteered" by DOSAAF or by their employers, Party and Komsomol secretaries, and trade-union organizations, and thus, as so often happens in the Soviet Union, are recruited on a "voluntary-compulsory" basis.[19] They receive their own training at civil defense schools, which the employed among them presumably attend on paid leave from their regular jobs. Although the local DOSAAF committee may provide special lectures, most instructors only train groups at their own place of employment, school, or residence. The number of people trained by a single instructor varies considerably. Instructors who have taught 250 persons receive awards, and some are reported to have trained more than 1,000 persons,[20] but most of them teach only between 100 and 200 persons. The Soviets have published no figures on the total number of instructors, but fragmentary information points to the existence of large numbers of them. To list only a few such partial data from recent years: the Leningrad Institute of Water Transport Engineering (with 1,500 students and teachers) had twenty-five civil defense training circles; the Moscow Agricultural Academy had 600 instructors; the "Zavodstroi" plant in Dzerzhinsk had 250 instructors; a factory in Kolchugino had 225; there were 2,756 women instructors in Kiev in 1959; the Armenian Republic trained 14,000 instructors in 1958 alone; one city district of Tashkent had 1,400 instructors; the city of Uralsk had 300 instructors for training apartment-house managers; a rural district of the Pskov region had 200 instructors; and another, in the Kursk region, had 300 instructors.[21]

The training consists of a series of lectures and, increasingly since 1958, of training exercises. Lectures are supplemented by a large and growing supply of pamphlets and books, films, slides, charts, and other visual aids, provided by the local DOSAAF (see fig. 3).[22] Training equipment for practical exercises will vary according to the civil defense course of the moment. According to a Soviet manual, the current course requires each training circle to use the accompanying list of equipment.

4 crowbars
6 shovels
2 levers
2 hooks
4 brooms
3 medical stretchers
1 collapsible stretcher
2 hammock stretchers
100 feet of rope
1 dummy
3 first-aid kits
9 simplified first-aid kits
12 packets of bandages
1 or 2 ladders
2 axes
1 basket
5 carrier straps
Gas masks for all trainees
A number of protective rubberized antichemical suits with gloves, boots, and hoods
1 to 4 fire hoses
Some chemical fire extinguishers
1 to 2 bucket extinguisher pumps
5 to 7 buckets
Individual decontamination packets for all trainees
Atropine syrettes
2 sets of warning signs for contaminated areas
Several dosimeters and radiation meters
Several chemical detector kits
Materials to simulate fires, contamination, and decontaminants.[23]

In addition, many localities have chambers for testing gas masks and teaching their use in the presence of gas (usually chloropicrin).[24] Mobile exhibits and film projection units are sent to the villages to publicize civil defense and help to train the rural population through civil defense films.[25]

Since training is compulsory and is conducted in small local circles, the Soviet authorities have little need of the mass propaganda media either to popularize the program or to train the population. Only rarely are civil defense lectures given over the radio or television. In rural areas, civil defense films are sometimes shown after the regular feature, but this rarely happens in the large cities. Occasional civil defense posters show the various phases of the training program in factories or offices, and there are also a number of civil defense exhibits, including a permanent one in Moscow. Otherwise, the sporadic training exercises, the published civil defense books and pamphlets, and possibly DOSAAF newspapers and magazines reporting on the progress and shortcomings of the training program are about the only evidence of civil defense training that foreign travelers in the USSR are likely to see.

The Training Courses

Since 1955, when the postwar civil defense training program was launched, there have been four compulsory civil defense training courses, which by 1962 will add up to 64 hours of training for the individual citizen. The entire program can be divided into two phases, one antedating the Fourth All-Union DOSAAF Congress of 1958 and the other following it. Whereas the earlier courses were largely theoretical in character, those since 1958 have emphasized practical training and exercises and also seemingly involve more people than did the earlier series. All the training courses have tended to cover the same subjects, but the emphasis has varied.

1. FIRST COURSE, 1955–1956

The first compulsory postwar course, instituted in mid-1955 and to be completed in 1956, required 10 hours of classwork. It concentrated on civil defense measures against attacks with atomic weapons and, consequently, was called "PAZ," which stood for *Protivoatomnaia Zashchita* ("Anti-Atomic Defense").[26]

In addition to describing the nature and effects of atomic as well as conventional weapons, and the various means of delivering them, the course dealt with the individual means of protection—gas masks, shelters, blackout, medical first aid to casualties, fire-fighting, rescue, and decontamination—and taught people how to respond to various civil defense warning signals.[27]

In theory, everyone between the ages of 16 and 60 was compelled to take the course, and Tolstikov has claimed that "during 1955–1956, 85.5 per cent of the entire population was trained."[28] This would mean, however, that about 110 million persons in the USSR had passed the course, and there is no evidence to support this claim. It is probable that a large percentage of DOSAAF members was required to take the course, and that self-defense groups, some industrial workers, and a limited number of others were also exposed to it. The figure cited by Tolstikov may possibly be correct for the DOSAAF membership alone, but neither this nor any subsequent course is likely to have involved as many participants as he has claimed.

2. SECOND COURSE, 1956–1958

In 1956, DOSAAF announced a second, 22-hour training course. Its program differed from the preceding one in that it included discussion of bacteriological weapons and provided more systematic coverage of chemical weapons.[29] The DOSAAF press also indicates that some exercises in the use of gas masks and fire-fighting were conducted, and greater attention seems to have been paid to the use of shelters.[30]

After Marshal Zhukov's public endorsement of the training program in his speech before the Twentieth Party Congress in 1956, the training was extended to a larger number of people than before. Although the major stress was still on the training of DOSAAF members and industrial workers, efforts were also made to enlist other urban and rural elements. According to the Soviet press, the majority of the large cities completed the course by mid-1958, but training often lagged behind elsewhere, and especially in rural areas.[31] There were complaints of shortages of qualified instructors and of training materials.[32] In many districts the course was not completed until the end of 1959. Despite serious shortcomings, however, many reports claim the successful completion of the training by factories, villages, cities, rural districts, and entire republics. According to the Soviet press, the course was completed by the "entire adult population" of sixty districts of the Belorussian Republic, by 85 per cent of all adults in the Kirgiz Republic, and by every adult in the Ukrainian Republics, the Tatar Autonomous Republic, the regions of Gorki, Sverdlosk, and others.[33] Undoubtedly, some DOSAAF committees inflated the number of trainees under their jurisdiction, and the quality of the training was frequently poor. Nevertheless, many millions of Soviet citizens apparently passed this second, 22-hour training course.

3. THIRD COURSE, 1958–1960

The training program changed in scope, and to some extent in character, after the meeting of the Fourth All-Union DOSAAF Congress in early 1958. The congress stressed the importance of civil defense training, ordered the completion of the current 22-hour course, and approved another (14-hour) course for the entire adult population of the country. The new course called for extensive practical work, and the trainees were to be examined on their knowledge in the eight subjects, or "norms," into which the course was divided. On passing the examinations, the student would receive the badge "Ready for Anti-Air Defense, First Grade," and the course itself came to be known by that name.[34] Concerning this new program, the deputy chief of the Civil Defense Administration and Technical

Training of the DOSAAF Central Committee, Zapolskii, wrote at the time of the congress meeting:

The character of the civil defense training of the DOSAAF society members and of the population has now become more complex owing to the fact that the resolutions of the Congress have placed new problems before the DOSAAF organizations.

At this time the training of the population in civil defense must consist of the following three parts: for the entire population—training in the norms "Ready for PVO," First Grade and passing these norms; for the DOSAAF members—familiarization with and advanced studies of a series of problems that formerly had not been included in the training programs of civil defense study circles; organization and the holding of civil defense competitions in order to fix in the memory of the participants the acquired knowledge and inculcate in them practical skill.[35]

Instructors had to be trained or retrained in line with the new orientation of the course, and more equipment and space had to be provided. With the changed emphasis on practical training, including the use of shelters, the civil defense authorities had to procure and distribute various items of equipment in large numbers and issue new manuals.

The eight "norms" of the course, and the final examinations on them, covered theoretical as well as practical knowledge. Those who failed to pass the tests were supposed to repeat the course. The descriptive titles of the individual norms, details of which are given in Appendix A, are listed below:[36]

Present methods of attack and characteristics and effects of atomic, chemical, and bacteriological weapons (one hour);

Individual means of protection and practice in the use of gas masks (one hour);

Collective means of protection and correct methods of operating shelter equipment (two hours);

Fire prevention and fire-fighting (one hour);

Civil defense warning signals and actions to be taken in response to each of them (two hours);

Medical first aid (three hours);

Post-attack operations, including the detection of contamination, decontamination procedures, and behavior in contaminated areas (two hours);

Veterinary aid to livestock and protection of livestock (two hours)—this training to be given only in rural areas.

The course and the manuals provided fairly detailed descriptions of the types of weapons to which the population might be exposed in an enemy attack. Trainees were told the characteristics and shown pictures of such U.S. strategic bombers as the B-52, B-36, and B-47, and the British V bombers, as well as of some American and British tactical and fighter planes.[37] They were also told the characteristics and performance of U.S. missiles such as the Matador, Navaho, Snark, Corporal, Atlas, Rascal, Jupiter, Redstone, and Thor.[38]

The trainees were also taught in some detail the principles of fusion and fission, how atomic and hydrogen weapons work, their explosive equivalents in terms of TNT, the different ways of exploding nuclear weapons (air, surface, underground, and underwater), and the effects of nuclear explosions (blast, thermal radiation, direct radiation, and fallout). Manuals and exhibits frequently showed pictures of Nagasaki and Hiroshima and of victims of those explosions—eloquent illustrations of some of the dangers to which the Soviet population would be exposed in the event of a war.[39]

Although seemingly liberal with technical and pictorial data on nuclear weapons effects, however, the third course, like the earlier ones, withheld some important information. The description of weapon effects dealt only with nominal atomic weapons of the Hiroshima type, whose explosion was equivalent to 20 kilotons (i.e., 20,000 tons of TNT). Concerning hydrogen bombs, the manuals said only that their explosive power was greater than that of atomic weapons. On radioactive fallout, too, the manuals were very misleading, giving the impression that the area of dangerous fallout would be in the shape of an irregular ellipse, which could stretch for "tens of kilometers."[40] (In practice, of course, fallout will vary according to weather conditions and the size of the weapon: downwind, in the event of a ground detonation, it is likely to extend over several hundred miles—or 1.6 times that many kilometers.)

Although many of the 1958 manuals still played down the effects of hydrogen weapons and fallout, others, more realistic in their treatment of these subjects, were published by the Ministry of Defense. A book entitled *Thermonuclear Weapons* described the U. S. Bikini tests and their fallout patterns.[41] One manual, which also dealt with the area of the Bikini fallout, mentioned that the United States had tested bombs of 1–15 megatons (equivalent to 1–15 million tons of TNT) and was considering using 5-megaton weapons against enemy cities in the event of a war.[42] Several books said that the fallout area stretched for 100–200 miles from the point of explosion.[43] Despite this trend toward greater realism, however, the 1958–1960 training course, in general, avoided giving all known details about the effects of hydrogen weapons and the probable size of the fallout areas. Apparently, Soviet civil defense authorities were anxious not to alarm the population too much or to weaken the public's confidence in the civil defense measures. But even in its restricted form, the information could not fail to be impressive. It is probable that for most people the pictures of Hiroshima and Nagasaki alone were eloquent enough.

The course and manuals also paid considerable attention to chemical and bacteriological weapons; as in the instruction concerning nuclear weapons, the trainees were shown photographs or colored drawings of the effects of some of these weapons on people.[44] Yperite, lewisite, nitrogen-mustard, phosgene, diphosgene, chloracetophenone, adamsite, hydrocyanic acid, prussic acid, cyanogenchloride, tabun, and sarin were the chemical agents mentioned most frequently. Among bacteriological agents, the manuals listed bubonic and pneumonic plague, tularemia, glanders, brucellosis, anthrax, melioidosis, cholera, botulism, typhus, psittacosis, smallpox, yellow fever, histoplasmosis, coccidiomycosis, tsutsugamushi, hoof-and-mouth disease, cattle plagues, and crop pests.[45] Instructors were directed, when discussing chemical weapons, to emphasize the nerve gases, such as tabun and sarin,[46] and in their first-aid classes to teach the use of atropine syrettes, an antidote against such gases.[47] Moreover, the trainees not only learned how to put on gas masks and protective clothing in the shortest possible time, but also tested the masks in gas chambers and practiced wearing them at work or on hikes.[48]

Conventional and radiological weapons also received some attention. The latter were described as highly radioactive agents, derived from nuclear waste, which could be delivered in the form of dusts, sprays, or smokes and could contain radioactive elements with half-lives of from one to more than three months so as to ensure the contamination of an area for a protracted period of time.[49]

The training in first aid emphasized medical self-help and mutual assistance. On the grounds that at Hiroshima and Nagasaki many persons who suffered burns, wounds from flying debris, electric shocks from broken high-tension wires, and other injuries had died because of lack of prompt medical help, the training was oriented toward the quick treatment of burns, shock, broken bones, bleeding, and similar injuries by nonmedical personnel. It ignored the treatment of radiation sickness, which requires blood transfusions and more elaborate equipment and expert medical attention.

In general, the course aimed at teaching people how to behave in the event of an attack, and what reasonable, relatively effective, and yet fairly simple and cheap measures they could employ to increase their chances of survival and reduce the hazards and damages of such an attack.

The 14-hour course, like the preceding one, met with difficulties and uneven results. Instructors were often in short supply or inadequately trained, and there were many instances of shortages of equipment, of poor utilization of the available equipment, of apathetic officials, and of officials who filed inflated reports about the number of trainees.[50] Many areas, especially cities, nevertheless claimed to have completed the training program on time, while others, particularly rural districts, admittedly lagged behind.

DOSAAF press reports on the progress of the course, divided fairly evenly between praise and criticism, did much to correct the shortcomings and to spur on the lagging organizations. In the Soviet Union, more so than in the West, criticism in the press exercises very strong pressure on officials, since the press is an instrument of the higher authorities whose views can be ignored only at some peril. Thus, despite a late start in many areas that had to await completion of the earlier course before embarking on the 14-hour course, DOSAAF was able to announce on February 12, 1961, that "the majority of the organizations of our voluntary patriotic society have successfully completed training the population in the course 'Ready for Anti-Air Defense, First Grade.' "[51]

4. FOURTH COURSE, 1960–1961

Toward the end of 1959, it was announced that a new (18-hour) mass training course was to follow the 14-hour course in 1960. It would emphasize practical ways of dealing with the effects of nuclear, chemical, and bacteriological attack, and qualified trainees would receive the badge "Ready for Anti-Air Defense, 2nd Grade." The course was divided into six norms and included a final three-hour examination. The express purpose of the training was not merely as before to "teach each citizen individual actions of self-protection," but to "inculcate in the population practical knowledge in carrying out simple work for dealing with the effects of an attack from the air, individually and as a part of the mass units of the MPVO."[52]

The headings of the norms are descriptive of their content[53] (for details, see Appendix B):

Purpose and function of the MPVO and methods of protecting the population against fallout (two hours);

Use of shelters and methods of rescue and repair work in disaster areas (three hours);

Fire-fighting under difficult conditions (two hours);

Methods of searching for casualties, first aid, and evacuation of casualties (four hours);

Operations in contaminated areas, including detection of radioactive, chemical, and bacteriological agents, and decontamination procedures (four hours);

Theoretical and practical examination of the trainees (three hours).

In addition to lectures, the course included up to forty practical demonstrations and exercises.

Compared to the previous courses, the 1960–1961 course was far more realistic about the character of the nuclear threat and no longer played down the danger from fallout. Civil defense instructors told their students that fallout might extend over "hundreds of kilometers" from the point of a nuclear explosion.[54] It was admitted that nuclear weapons of considerable size might be used against the Soviet Union, and mention was made of the performance and effects of thermonuclear weapons up to 20 megatons.[55] However, as before, genetic and other long-term effects of nuclear explosions were not discussed.

Another novel feature of this latest course was the information it contained on the organization and procedures of evacuation, which was described as "one of the most important measures instituted for the protection of the population."[56] Evacuation, which will be discussed in detail in a separate chapter, had been ignored by Soviet civil defense until 1958, and thereafter had been mentioned only in general terms.[57]

The 1960–1961 course also included for the first time training in the use of dosimeters, radiation meters, and chemical detector kits.[58] Furthermore, the trainees were to be taken to their nearest shelters to learn how to operate shelter equipment and to practice rescue operations.[59] As was noted earlier, this novel emphasis on practical work prompted the establishment of numerous civil defense schools and special training areas.

In addition to the general course, some members of DOSAAF receive specialized training. Truck and motorcycle drivers, for example, are taught also how to decontaminate their vehicles.[60] Under the plan, DOSAAF was to train at least 2 million truck, tractor, and motorcycle drivers in 1961.[61] It is probable that some of these drivers would be used by the Civil Defense Transport Service in an emergency.

There are also special civil defense courses for those not subject to the regular training program. Men above the age of 60 and women above 55 are given lectures and shown films or slides; school children between the ages of 12 and 16 are taught the use of gas masks and protective clothing, first aid, and also individual methods of protection and of decontamination.[62]

The 18-hour training course, like the previous ones, is apparently meeting with some difficulties. In some areas, instructors are inadequately trained; in others, there are complaints that the trainees are not being given the required practical experience or are suffering from a shortage of training aids.[63] In a number of instances, existing training equipment is not being used, even though, as one magazine article stated, "there are now available large quantities of dosimeters and chemical detector kits, intended for reconnaissance work."[64]

Despite these shortcomings, however, and the usual lag especially in rural districts, the course on the whole seems to be meeting its schedule, particularly in cities and industrial installations. In general, the quality and scope of the training appear to have been improved, more equipment is available, and DOSAAF is making a considerable effort to overcome the shortcomings and spur on the lagging areas.

The Soviet press contains no evidence of any country-, republic-, or region-wide civil defense exercises. Except for city-wide exercises in a few cities such as Elektrostal (Moscow *oblast*), Blagoveshchensk (Khabarovsk *oblast*), and Zhdanov (Ukraine), and those observed by travelers in a few smaller towns, the press reports only factory or city-block exercises and drills by individual self-defense teams throughout the USSR.[65]

The only exercises that are mentioned frequently are the so-called *spartakiada,* in which civil defense teams publicly compete with one another and are graded according to the correctness and speed with which they complete various civil defense exercises. These competitions, which may be at any level from local to national, at times include many thousands of participants.[66]

Scope and Cost of the Training Program

The Soviet press gives no indication of the number of persons who participated in the last two training courses, beyond the initial announcement that they were to be taken by the "majority" of the adult population. If one were to credit the claims of some regional or republic DOSAAF committees to the effect that about 80 per cent of the population in their areas had received civil defense instruction, and if one took this to be typical of the nationwide average, this would mean that some 100.5 million persons in the Soviet Union had been trained—an unlikely number in view of the admitted shortcomings of the program. The Soviet press does indicate, however, that the courses have been attended by the majority of the more than 30 million DOSAAF members, as well as by members of the Red Cross, large numbers of industrial workers, and many other persons, including office workers, housewives, and farmers. A plausible estimate of the number of people who attended the latest training courses might be at least 50 million, and the total number trained thus far, at somewhere between 50 and 100 million. Among the participants, urban residents probably outnumber farmers, and among the former there are doubtless more workers than housewives. (The number of housewives is relatively small in the Soviet Union, where a majority of married women are employed while their children are being raised by grandparents or in nurseries.)

Since the Soviet authorities have published no information on the cost of the training program, one can only make very tentative estimates of its possible range. In view of the increasing complexity and growing scope of the program, it is likely that Soviet expenditures have increased with each new course.

Even though neither instructors nor trainees were paid for their classwork, the cost of the 18-hour course for 1960–1961, for example, included expenditures for instructor training, equipment and training aids, training space and facilities, and administrative overhead. Based on Soviet prices for the various commodities involved, a tentative estimate of the annual total expenditure on this course (possibly on the conservative side, since it assumes a higher degree of efficiency in the use of instructors and equipment than is likely to exist in practice) would amount to about 100 million dollars for 50 million trainees, or 200 million dollars for 100 million trainees.* Of course, as noted earlier, DOSAAF and the MPVO would bear only a part of this cost.

* This calculation is based on an estimated 25 persons per study circle, and on the assumption that every instructor taught between 200 and 300 hours per year after having himself passed a 36-hour training course for which he received 250 rubles. The total costs also include the pay of teachers who train the instructors, initial training equipment in the amount of $650 for every study circle, the cost of replacing equipment, and administrative expenditures. (The author is indebted to Mrs. Doris Iklé of The RAND Corporation for her assistance in preparing these cost estimates.)

Controls and Enforcement

Although participation in the training courses is supposedly compulsory, Soviet literature does not make it clear how attendance is enforced. The July 2, 1941, decree on universal compulsory training for the adult population of the USSR, which is still in force, does not specify penalties for those who disobey.[67] Local directives issued during the war on the basis of this decree threatened defaulters with punishment under the severe wartime laws.[68]

More recently, however, psychological, social, and even economic pressures are the preferred means of enforcing compliance with the training requirement. The Soviet system is, of course, so organized as to permit control of the citizens' behavior. Pressure is exercised through the local Party organization at a person's place of work or residence, through the management at his place of employment, by the trade-union organization, and finally through his coworkers and neighbors. It succeeds not only in enforcing approved social behavior but also in raising the quality and quantity of production. At work, the Soviet citizen is a member of his shop, office, or work brigade and is expected to support the efforts of that team. His coworkers, on instructions from the Party or Komsomol representative, can exert great pressure through public criticism, whatever the issue. For example, if the shop is engaged in a competition that promises larger bonuses for members of the winning team, the performance of every shopworker becomes a matter of personal concern to his colleagues. If he is a member of the Party or Komsomol, these organizations will ensure that he does not default. Finally, the plant management can exercise great economic pressure on the worker by threatening not only dismissal but withholding of pay raises or, worse still, the loss of a treasured apartment, the scarcest commodity in the Soviet Union.

With these ever-present threats and pressures, compliance with the civil defense training rule usually requires only an admonishing word. Thus, the press reports the case of two workers at the railway depot of Novosibirsk who had failed to attend the training meetings: the instructor complained to the chief of the depot's reserve railway car section, and he, in turn, went to the local Komsomol committee, which summoned the culprits and told them: "How is this? The shop is competing for the right to be called a shop of Communist labor; each of us has promised to be highly conscientious, while you permit yourself to defame our workers' honor."[69] Not surprisingly, the offenders thereafter became model civil defense trainees. In another instance where two workers avoided classes, the instructor "made it so hot for them" at a shop meeting that they quickly mended their ways.[70] The successful manipulation of moral pressures, however, does not exclude the possibility that the Soviet authorities will resort to legal punitive sanctions in dealing with those who persistently evade civil defense training, as appears to be the case in some of the satellite countries.[71]

Popular Attitude toward the Training Program

Even if the authorities can enforce course attendance, it is quite another problem for them to control the popular attitude toward civil defense training. The psychological effect of the preoccupation with civil defense is twofold and contradictory. On the one hand, civil defense activity tends to raise people's anxiety by stressing the possibility of war and the destructiveness of modern weapons. On the other hand, it attempts to reassure them about their chances of surviving a war. Even though the leadership asserts that the Soviet Union would survive a nuclear war, it has also acknowledged that the country would suffer severe damage. To most Soviet citizens, who experienced World War II on their own territory, this official image of war is frightening enough to cause some apathy toward or lack of confidence in civil defense.

There is no indication that the institution of the training program as such has significantly alarmed the Soviet population or increased its expectation of war. The Soviet program has not been a crash effort, and its initiation was not connected with any specific crisis. Rather, the attempt has been to develop a civil defense capability at a steadily growing rate. The program has thus acquired a routine character and the majority of the population appear to accept it as a matter of course. This casual attitude is probably reinforced by the fact that the present effort is, in a sense, an extension of the earlier, prewar civil defense programs in which many Soviet citizens had participated.

At the same time, Khrushchev's public statements about the horrors of a future war, and the fairly detailed and increasingly realistic descriptions of modern weapons effects in the training courses, have not been without effect. An article published in 1958 complained: "Unfortunately, a certain though, it is true, insignificant part of the population still has not overcome the backward attitude that there is supposedly no escape from the atom bomb, and that allegedly there is therefore no point in studying in civil defense circles."[72] Still more recent press accounts reveal that instructors often meet with similar attitudes on the part of their trainees, who ask: "Why is all this necessary? When the atom bomb goes off, nothing can help."[73] Among the statements quoted are "I guess there is no place to hide from an atomic explosion,"[74] and, "The atom bomb—that is a clever thing. If it gets hold of you, watch out."[75] Naturally, the reports cite these incidents chiefly in order to show how the instructors overcame these fears and convinced their audiences that civil defense could provide effective protection against such weapons.

It is impossible to know just how widespread those defeatist sentiments may be, but it is safe to say that the training program probably has not succeeded in overcoming them. For many Russians, the attitude toward war appears to be determined not only by the question of their own physical survival but also by their fear of seeing the destruction of the factories and homes that they built by making great sacrifices and enduring many hardships. Some people probably are reassured by the civil defense program, but for most Soviet citizens the memory of World War II is sufficiently recent and vivid to make them fear war, be it conventional or nuclear.

The Soviet authorities are also faced with the problem of simple apathy or lack of interest. There have been complaints that some trainees merely came to the meetings to register their attendance and did not sit through the classwork.[76] This is likely to have been especially true during the first two courses, which did not require practical exercises. Some people reportedly attended the meetings "with bored expressions and sat close to the exit."[77] Others apparently were annoyed by the repetitiousness of the courses. Some women objected to being included in the training program at all. In one of the study circles, a girl who appeared to act as spokesman for the group is said to have asked the instructor: "Tell us, Dilbar, why are you giving us all this? Really we don't intend to fight. And besides, we are women."[78] The DOSAAF committees have tried to overcome this indifference by making the classes more interesting, though we have no way of knowing to what extent they have succeeded. Threatening those who fail the course with having to repeat it might be effective, but there is no information on whether or not this rule is being enforced.

Although these negative accounts are balanced by numerous reports of enthusiastic participation in the courses, of farmers and housewives writing to DOSAAF committees about their eagerness to share in the training program, and of the excellent quality of the training in many areas of the Soviet Union, substantial numbers of trainees undoubtedly remain apathetic or bored. Nevertheless, the very repetitiousness of the training course and the emphasis on its practical application are bound to leave a considerable residue of civil defense knowledge in the minds of most Soviet citizens, regardless of attitude. In time of crisis, their training will doubtless assert itself, and they can be expected to act in accordance with civil defense instructions.

4

Dispersal and City Planning

For a number of years, Soviet authorities have been concerning themselves with the related tasks of city planning and the dispersal of population and industry, and have taken certain steps in that direction. Although such measures are never officially associated with the requirements of civil defense or justified in those terms, they do, in fact, have considerable significance for the civil defense effort. If population and industry were less heavily concentrated, if urban congestion (and thus the urban fire hazard) were reduced, and if evacuation facilities could be improved, the likely degree of damage and number of casualties in the event of a war would be substantially lower than under present conditions.

Dispersal

The military importance of the dispersal of people and industry is frequently stressed in the Soviet Union. As mentioned earlier, Khrushchev and other Soviet officials have boasted that in these respects their country is more fortunate and hence less vulnerable to attack than the United States and other Western nations. According to one military writer: "A large territory makes it possible to disperse industry and the population with the aim of sheltering them from destruction by atomic weapons. In this respect our country, like other countries with relatively low population density, is in a more favorable position than the Western European states where the population density is very high."[1] Although the Soviet urban population is more heavily concentrated than this statement might lead one to believe, it is undeniably less so than the American. (For example, in 1959 the ten largest Soviet cities had a total of 17 million residents, whereas the ten largest metropolitan areas in the United States accounted for a total population of more than 40 million.) The Soviet urban planning authorities have attempted to restrict the growth of large cities and to reduce the population density in metropolitan areas. City planners reject as undesirable the development of enormous metropolitan areas similar to New York. The Chairman of the City Planning Commission of the USSR, V. Kucherenko, has declared: "This tendency [toward the unrestricted growth of large cities] must be decisively checked, and we have every possibility and every reason for doing so."[2]

One impediment to such growth in the USSR is the shortage of housing space. But urban growth is being deliberately curtailed by means of restrictions on residence permits and the controlled construction of new industry. Thus, after World War II the Soviet authorities sought to put a ceiling on Leningrad's population by limiting it to 97 per cent of its prewar size; and they prohibited the construction of new large factories within the city limits of Moscow.[3] The Chief of the City Planning and Construction Department of the USSR State Building Administration has stated: "The growth of large cities can most effectively be limited by discontinuing construction of industrial and other enterprises there. It was suggested that plants and factories, research institutes, teaching institutes, and colleges be located in small and medium-sized towns and communities."[4]

The Soviet authorities, therefore, are keenly interested in the development of new cities and towns. "Nine hundred new cities and thousands of urban communities" are said to have been

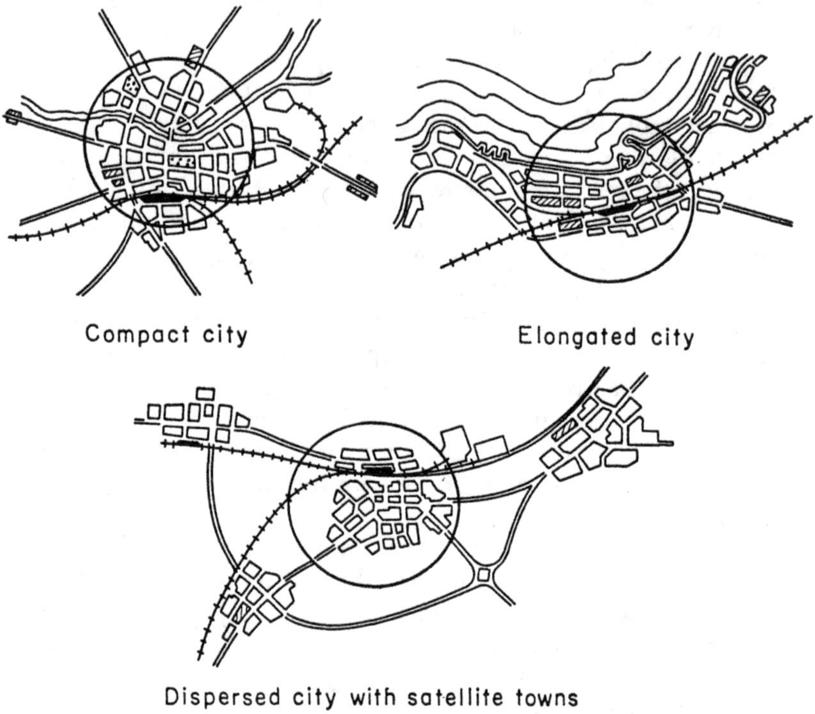

FIG. 4. Effect of city design on area of destruction.

built since 1917, including 118 new towns built between 1951 and 1956, and 200 between 1956 and 1959.[5] According to the planners, the ideal city should have a population of from 100,000 to 300,000.[6]

Soviet civil defense officials, and apparently also some of the political leaders, have acknowledged the connection between the population density and layout of a city and its vulnerability to attack. Current manuals point out that very compact cities, especially if they are on level ground and roughly circular in shape, will suffer greater damage than those that are more dispersed and elongated in form (see figure 4): ". . . cities that have a low population density and include a series of satellite towns, especially if they are located behind elevations, are better suited to the demands of anti-atomic defense, since the degree and character of damage that will occur will be in such instances significantly smaller."[7] Khrushchev supported this theory at the Twentieth Party Congress in 1956, and added specific practical suggestions:

> We know that the natural increase in the population of our cities is quite large . . . [and it is] desirable to spread out the population of large cities by building small, well-appointed townships around Moscow, Leningrad, Kiev, Kharkov, and other centers. . . . This means that good, well-appointed houses should be built not on the territory of the large cities themselves, but at a certain distance from them, creating such living conditions there that people would seek to move there. Some enterprises should be moved to such townships, so that people could work there.[8]

The idea of the satellite town has since received increasing attention and comment. The afore-mentioned Kucherenko, for example, has said:

> The limitation and reduction of size of the population in major cities can be accomplished by means of decentralizing the population.
>
> The satellite towns will be economically and functionally rational only if their construction coincides with that of industrial enterprises that will employ part of the residents.
>
> Calculations have shown that satellite towns, if they include industry, may be located 60–80 kilometers [37–50 miles] from large cities.[9]

This type of dispersal, the civil defense manuals point out, will reduce the vulnerability of an area and prevent the destruction of several important installations in a single attack.[10]

A number of satellite towns are now being planned around large cities, and some are actually under construction. Moscow will eventually have fourteen such towns, Leningrad six, and many other cities one or more. At least one such town now being built near Moscow will have a population of 65,000.[11]

The primary emphasis in the concept of industrial dispersal is not on the redistribution of existing production units, although Soviet planners agree that certain industries now located in large cities might well be moved to smaller towns;[12] rather, the trend seems to be toward economic regionalism, with special emphasis on the development of new industries in formerly underdeveloped regions of the Soviet Union, chiefly in Siberia. In the planning of new industrial sites, consideration is being given not only to economic factors but also to defense needs. Says one Soviet economic planner:

> The importance of more uniform distribution of industry is very great from the point of view of strengthening the defense potential of the USSR. The defense potential will be strengthened when [the Soviet Union] has numerous industrial bases, including some deep inside the country, and when local industry is developed extensively.... The fundamental requirements of defense in the distribution of industry... the location of enterprises deep within the country, and the creation of relatively dispersed industrial bases in various parts of the country... will be met by a more uniform distribution of industry, by having industry close to the sources of raw materials and to consuming regions, by the accelerated industrialization of national districts and formerly backward regions, and by the complex development of the economy in each economic region....
>
> The carrying-out of the requirements of socialist distribution in industry is tied to the rapid development of industry in the East, in regions possessing tremendous natural resources... [and] this movement of industry to the East fully coincides with defense needs.[13]

Although Soviet literature reports the development of new industrial centers and regions, it gives no clear indication of the extent of actual dispersal of industry. As the main emphasis is clearly on the location of new industries rather than on the relocation of existing ones, it is probable that little has been done to reduce the industrial concentration in large Soviet cities. Moreover, city planners, in choosing new locations, are finding it somewhat difficult to bring rational city planning into harmony with the civil defense requirements that factories be "dispersed at a sufficient distance from each other" so as to reduce their vulnerability.[14]

Beginning in the late 1950's, the Soviet Union also took certain steps toward administrative and economic decentralization that carry with them implications for civil defense. One of these was the establishment, in 1957, of "economic regions." This scheme was designed to produce a greater regional economic integration and a considerable dispersal of economic and industrial administrations that had previously been concentrated in Moscow. On this score, Khrushchev told a foreign correspondent: ". . . the reorganization of industry that we have carried out insures a more autonomous management of industry, which is also a strategic gain."[15]

A more recent move toward decentralization has been the abolition of the Ministry for Internal Affairs of the USSR and the transfer of some of its functions (notably, control over the regular police) to the constituent republic.[16] A possible future measure in the same direction, mentioned by Khrushchev, is the reorganization of the Soviet army on a territorial or militia system.[17] Although we cannot be certain that defense considerations played a decisive role in these developments, they probably entered into the picture. Administrative decentralization may be designed, at least in part, to ensure continuity of functions in the several regions of the USSR in the event that central administrative and political control and communications were to be disrupted by an enemy attack.

City Planning

Soviet construction and planning authorities have been seeking to develop a master urban development plan for the USSR. They insist that every city develop a comprehensive plan based on a specific set of principles, which include relieving the congestion in residential areas, providing for separate industrial districts, improving transportation, and promoting other features of modern urban development.

Part of the general endeavor to reduce urban vulnerability is a plan to remove dangerous industries and some vital installations from the cities.[18] New industries are to be located 6 to 9 miles away from residential districts of cities with more than 100,000 inhabitants, and will be separated from such districts by belts of parks and greenery.[19] Major communication installations are to be moved to the outskirts of large cities.[20]

Soviet civil defense manuals describe a variety of other measures that must be taken in peacetime to reduce urban vulnerability to military attack.

> Strengthening the more important buildings, structures, and the municipal and industrial electric power networks; the construction and planning of new buildings, inhabited districts, industrial centers, and populated points with consideration for anti-atomic defense requirements; the carrying-out of the more time-consuming fire-prevention measures; the technical camouflage and blackout of cities and of large installations of the people's economy; the protection of food supplies, water, and fodder; the construction and equipping of collective means of defense (shelters) and other measures.[21]

Many of these measures, it is pointed out, are most easily carried out during the planning and construction of new buildings, districts, or cities.[22]

Civil defense requirements in city planning include the construction of wide streets, which are less likely to be blocked by rubble than are narrow ones, and thus would facilitate evacuation and the movement of rescue teams after an attack.[23] The width of a street should be determined by the height of the buildings on either side. It is noteworthy that in the last few years the construction of very tall buildings has been prohibited and the maximum height for most Soviet buildings has been set at five stories.[24] Wide streets, parks, and belts of greenery are intended also: "To create barriers against the spread of fires and to keep evacuation routes free of debris while the effects of an atomic attack are being dealt with, zones planted with greenery (boulevards, parks) are laid out in populated places."[25]

Current plans call for "the planting of greenery in towns ... [as] a matter of national importance" and envisage that by 1965 every city will have 258 square feet of greenery per inhabitant.[26] Some cities, such as Omsk, already have as much as 750 square feet of park area for every resident.[27]

Other recommendations in the interest of civil defense include the construction of water, gas, and sewage systems at a considerable depth underground, and in such a way that damaged sections could be sealed off to permit the use of undamaged ones.[28] Also, the cities' transportation tunnels and other underground passages are to be "adapted for the evacuation of casualties from the disaster area."[29]

Naturally, such measures are most easily instituted in new districts or cities. In Moscow, therefore, plans for the rehabilitation and expansion of the city aim at reducing population density by calling for 50 per cent of all new housing to be built in new areas on the city's periphery.[30] Between 1960 and 1965, about 70,000 new apartments are to be built in such areas.[31] The new Moscow districts, some of which are already completed, will have broad avenues, some over 300 feet wide, and considerably more greenery than the older sections, and buildings are more widely spaced than formerly.[32] Despite the ban on creating supermetropolitan areas, however, the Soviet authorities decided in 1960 to incorporate a large part of Moscow's outskirts into the city, thereby increasing its population from 5.5 million to about 7 million.[33] Partly, this may have been designed to simplify planning and administrative control in the Moscow region; quite possibly, also, the leadership was anxious to make Moscow appear statistically as one of the largest cities in the world.

The development of new districts in other cities is very similar to that in Moscow. The current Seven Year Plan calls for the construction of 15 million apartments, designed to house at least 45 million persons, that is to say, about 45 per cent of the total urban population.[84]

It would be difficult to say to what extent Soviet city planning and industrial dispersal are being prompted or influenced by civil defense considerations. Nearly all the measures planned or actually taken also serve purposes unrelated to civil defense. In all likelihood, the interests of civil defense have been taken into account wherever they coincided with other desirable features of city planning and where their implementation was relatively cheap and simple. Whether and to what extent this development will succeed in reducing Soviet urban vulnerability is difficult to predict. Without question, industrial dispersal is desirable as a means of preserving industries in the event of a war, and some of the measures cited above could facilitate evacuation or help to limit the spread of fires. On the other hand, even those plans that are technically feasible can hardly be fully realized in the near future. Moreover, it would be too expensive and too difficult to redesign existing large cities or to undertake drastic relocations of their industrial facilities. New towns and districts, though they may have the desired civil defense features, are likely to be much smaller and less important than the existing major centers. Furthermore, the inevitably slow process of urban renewal is especially difficult to carry out in the Soviet Union, with its chronic housing shortage and crowded living conditions. No matter how concerned the leadership may be about the cities' vulnerability to attack, it cannot attempt any redistribution of industry and population without seriously disrupting existing economic programs. The various dispersal measures could have a noticeable impact in the long run, but some of their benefits might be offset by the growing yields of nuclear weapons, whose increasing areas of devastation could nullify or render inadequate many of the current Soviet efforts to reduce urban vulnerability.

5

Individual Means of Protection

Soviet civil defense places great stress on the value of individual means of protection against chemical and bacteriological weapons and, to a lesser degree, against radioactive agents. The training program devotes considerable time to the characteristics of chemical and bacteriological weapons and to the various ways of countering their effects, and appreciable investments are being made in individual protective devices against such weapons.

The primary purpose of such devices is to protect face, eyes, respiratory organs, and the rest of the body against chemical and bacteriological agents. But they are also designed to protect the skin, eyes, nose, and mouth against radioactive dust or particles that might cause ulcerating sores and contribute to radiation sickness.[1] Although admittedly less reliable than shelters, these devices are described as essential for anyone who is out in the open in contaminated areas, either accidentally or of necessity. Soviet operational doctrine, as we shall see, envisages large-scale rescue and evacuation operations in the disaster area soon after an attack, and individual means of protection are therefore essential for rescuers and rescued alike.

A recent authoritative Soviet manual states:

> The more reliable defense of a large number of people against means of attack from the air, including also the effects of poisonous and radioactive matter, as well as against disease-causing microbes, is achieved through special defense structures of the MPVO—shelters equipped with filtration-ventilation facilities.
> But during an attack from the air the hermetic protection of these installations may be destroyed; the filtration-ventilation system may become inoperative. Furthermore, a part of the population will be forced to seek cover in simple types of shelter, which are not provided with antichemical defense devices. In all such instances, as well as when leaving a disaster area, it is essential to use individual means of protection for the respiratory organs and the skin.[2]

The best protection of respiratory organs, eyes, and face against chemical and bacteriological agents, as well as against radioactive fallout, is the gas mask.[3]

The latest civilian gas mask produced in the USSR is a filter type (model "GP-4U"), which is equipped with an antismoke filter, an antidust filter, an activated charcoal filter, and a chemical filter. Paper, cloth, or other mechanical filters may be used to cover the outside of the cartridge to provide additional protection against radioactive particles.[4] The mask has a special double-valve exhaust system that precludes accidental inhaling of chemical or bacteriological agents, some of which are lethal even in minute quantity.

The new mask (introduced in 1957 as an improvement over the similar model "GP-4," which had been in production for many years[5]) comes in three sizes for adults and two sizes for children under fourteen; special protective bags are said to be available for infants.[6] Civil defense also makes use of a military mask, which differs from the civilian varieties in that it does not stop at the hairline but covers the entire head.[7] Special self-contained oxygen masks, similar to those used in diving, are designed for use in highly contaminated areas where ordinary gas masks are not adequate and the user must rely on bottled oxygen.[8]

Although only gas masks are called truly reliable, the manuals list certain substitute protective devices (such as dust masks) to be used in an emergency, and the people are taught how to prepare these. For example, pieces of cloth or gauze containing

FIG. 5. Protective clothing.

wads of absorbent cotton may be tied over the mouth and nose; if cut into the shape of a mask, they can cover the entire face.[9]

Recent Soviet civil defense literature reveals interest also in protecting livestock against chemical, bacteriological, and radioactive agents. For cattle and horses, some special gas masks are said to be available; where they are not provided, the farmers are instructed to prepare emergency masks made of several layers of impregnated cloth.[10]

Under present policy, gas masks in peacetime are distributed only to civil defense personnel and for training purposes; the general population is to receive them only when the Soviet government believes there is danger of war.[11] The authorities probably fear that in the hands of many people the equipment

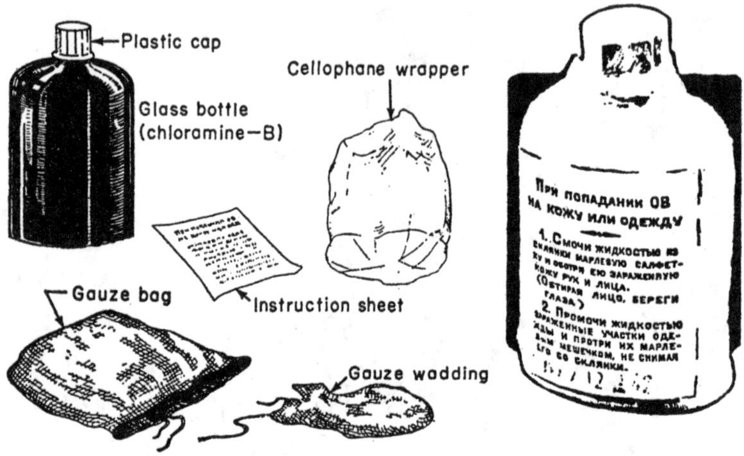

Fig. 6. Individual decontamination packet, IPP-5.

would suffer damage or abuse, but it is also possible that there simply are not enough masks on hand to equip the entire population.

For the protection of the skin and body, there is a variety of special suits, capes, hoods, gloves, leggings, and boots, usually of rubberized, plastic, or impregnated cloth; the protective cape is made of paper.[12] The most effective of the four standard types of protective clothing (see fig. 5) is a one-piece suit of rubberized cloth, complete with hood, rubber boots, and gloves, to be worn by civil defense workers in contaminated areas. Those less dangerously exposed will use lighter clothing.

For the present, the Soviet authorities intend to distribute protective clothing only to regular civil defense personnel. The average citizens, while being taught the importance and proper use of such protective garments, are advised to make their own suits, capes, and leggings from smooth cloth, preferably white.[13] Those who are caught unprepared are urged to use whatever material is at hand (gloves, coats, blankets, hats, stockings, boots, and so forth) in order to cover all exposed parts of the body. Worn in conjunction with gas masks, such clothing will provide some protection against bacteriological agents and against direct body contact with chemical and radioactive agents, but admittedly it will not shield people against certain toxic gases or against gamma radiation.[14]

Under the Soviet civil defense program, the general public is to be provided with individual chemical decontamination packets. As noted earlier, the people are already being trained in the use of these emergency packets, which are designed for the removal of liquid vesicants (agents causing burns or blistering) from the skin and clothing, and of radioactive dust from the body. The two models now available (see figs. 6 and 7) both contain a decontaminant solution (chloramine-B in aqueous alcohol) and gauze waddings or pads. The more complex model IPP-3 also has four inhalant ampules against smoke and specific chemical agents.[15]

The population is also being trained in the use of atropine syrettes for nerve gases, amylnitrite ampules for hydrocyanic gases, and antidote ampules for adamsite.[16] At least some of these antidotes may be included in the individual decontamination packets.

The Soviet authorities have given no indication of the number of individual means of protection that have been produced or distributed. The many press photographs of civil defense units wearing gas masks and full rubberized suits suggest that masks and protective clothing have been distributed to civil defense units, including self-defense groups, throughout the country.

The current table of equipment for a typical self-defense group calls for gas masks for all members of the group, with four additional masks to be used by the medical teams in treating casualties, and for protective suits for 50 per cent of the

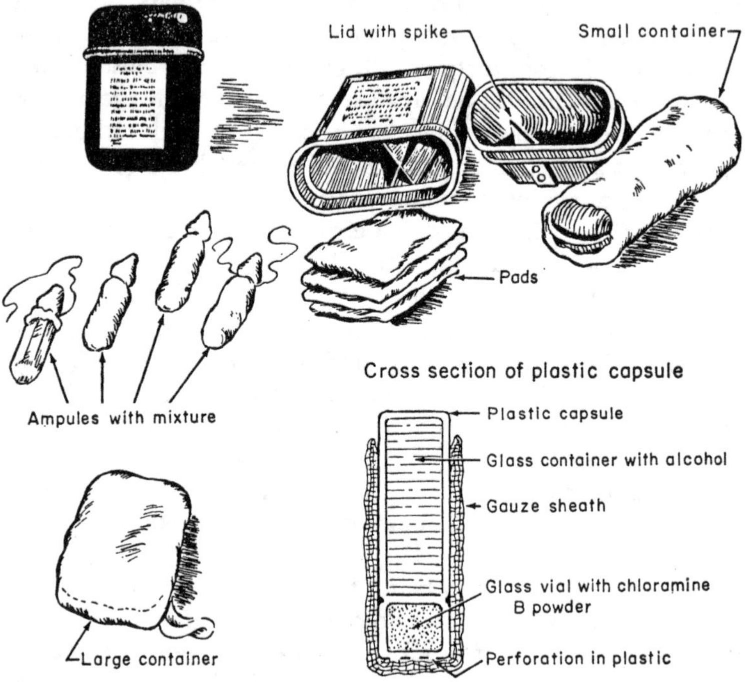

FIG. 7. Individual decontamination packet, IPP-3.

group; the veterinary team is to receive rubber boots, leggings, gloves, and aprons.[17] If, as Khrushchev claims, the Soviet civil defense organization has 22 million members, then presumably at least that many masks and some 10 million protective suits have been distributed.

In addition, each training group is supposed to have gas masks and individual decontamination packets for all participants, as well as several protective suits. Although in the past the Soviet press has occasionally complained of shortages of gas masks in some areas, it would appear from Soviet sources that most training groups today are provided with the requisite individual means of protection. This would mean that in addition to the equipment for civil defense personnel, several million additional gas masks and protective suits, and many millions of individual decontamination packets have been distributed for training purposes.

It is not known to what extent the Soviet government is manufacturing and stockpiling gas masks and other protective equipment, but the emphasis on gas-mask training in cities and rural areas, the public demonstrations to popularize the wearing of these masks, and the numerous photographs showing small-unit exercises with gas masks certainly suggest the intention of providing everyone with gas masks when needed. If the authorities had no such plan, they would probably deëmphasize the value of gas masks, rather than risk creating a popular demand for them in an emergency that could not be met. As it is, however, they seem prepared even to raise public apprehension about war by stressing the dangers created by chemical and bacteriological weapons. Moreover, people are told that in emergency fallout shelters, which will be built especially in the rural areas, they would have to wear gas masks, since such shelters could not be hermetically sealed.[18] As for other kinds of protective equipment, the authorities may continue to count on most people to improvise their own clothing, but they will have to make wide distribution of the personal decontamination packets if these are to be generally effective.

Nothing is known about expenditures on this program or about the production cost of individual items in the Soviet Union. The current U.S. prices for similar items would be about 12 dollars for a gas mask, 25 dollars for a full protective suit, and possibly 25 cents for an individual decontamination packet.* If we assume that the Soviet authorities so far have distributed between 20 and 30 million masks, 5 to 10 million suits, and possibly as many as 100 million decontamination packets, they will have spent, on the basis of U.S. prices, between 390 and 635 million dollars. A stockpile of enough gas masks for the entire population of 212 million, for example, would cost (again in U.S. prices) more than 2.5 billion dollars. If the Soviet gas mask were half the price of an American mask, such a program would still cost more than one billion dollars. And even if the actual cost of a Soviet mask were less than 6 dollars, it is obvious that the procurement of individual means of protection for a major part of the population would mean an expenditure of many millions of dollars. How much the government is actually spending on this kind of equipment, or has spent in the past, is difficult to ascertain. We do know, however, that the use of gas masks and of individual decontamination packets was described in Soviet civil defense manuals at least as early as 1951;[19] and protective clothing was mentioned in manuals published in 1955–1956 (and perhaps even earlier).[20] It is probable, therefore, that the Soviet authorities have by now stockpiled enough gas masks and other protective devices for at least a substantial part of the urban population.

* Prices provided by the Fire Department of Santa Monica, California.

6

Shelters

The Soviet authorities recognize that one of the more reliable means of protection against all types of weapons is the shelter.

To protect the people in cities and [other] inhabited places from all means of attack from the air, there are structures specially built or adapted for this purpose.... They include shelters and cover built into the basements of apartment houses and public and other buildings, and separate shelters unconnected with buildings. The tunnels and stations of the subway, underground passages, pedestrian and transportation tunnels, and other underground structures may also be used for shelter and cover.[1]

The effectiveness of a given shelter against modern weapons must be measured by the degree of protection it can provide against nuclear blast, heat, light-flash, direct radiation from the explosion, fallout, chemical and bacteriological agents, high temperatures resulting from large fires, and the weight of debris from demolished buildings. How well a shelter will shield its occupants against these hazards will depend on a combination of factors: the structural strength of the shelter, its depth, its airtightness, its equipment (filter ventilation, water, food, etc.) for long-term occupancy, and, of course, its distance from the point of explosion and the yield of the enemy's weapon. Soviet literature distinguishes between permanent and emergency shelters. The permanent shelters are built in peacetime and are designed for relatively long occupancy. They provide better protection than emergency shelters, which are of lighter construction and are built only when the government believes there is imminent danger of a war. Permanent shelters are to be found in cities and important industrial or economic centers; emergency shelters are designed primarily for rural areas that are likely to be fairly safe from nuclear blast.[2] Soviet shelters vary greatly in size, accommodating anywhere from twenty to several thousand persons.

The great majority of the shelters planned or in existence, especially the permanent kinds, are public shelters. Little interest is shown in promoting family shelters, even in the countryside, although persons in suburban and rural areas are free to build such facilities, some of which will be described below. The official neglect of voluntary shelters and small units is in keeping with Soviet urban development practices, which discourage individual building. Also, under Soviet conditions, private shelter construction is extremely difficult. Since shelter construction is thus primarily the responsibility of the government, the authorities are finding it relatively easy to develop a systematic program, for which they determine priorities and establish standards of design and quality.

All permanent shelters built thus far in the Soviet Union are designed to protect against direct radiation, fallout, heat, lightflash, fire, and chemical and bacteriological agents, and also, to varying degrees, against blast.[3] They include: (1) deep and heavy detached shelters, (2) detached shelters, (3) subways, and (4) basement shelters.

Deep and Heavy Detached Shelters

According to Soviet civil defense manuals, only the very deep or very heavy shelters can withstand the blast at or near the

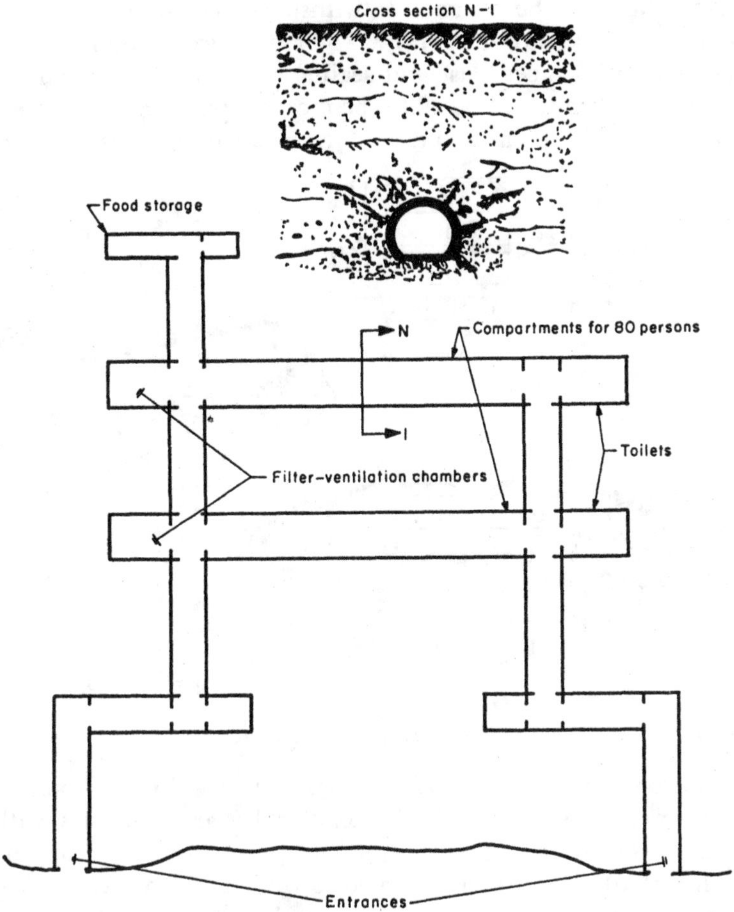

FIG. 8. Deep shelter.

point of a nuclear explosion.[4] Deep shelters are built in the form of networks of underground tunnels of reinforced concrete, a hundred or more feet below the surface of the ground, or as shafts in the side of hills and mountains (see fig. 8).[5] They are believed to be designed to withstand blast in excess of 300 pounds per square inch (psi).[6] Their filter ventilation systems, water, toilets, steel blast and sealing doors, food, communication equipment, and possibly chemical air purifiers and bottled oxygen render them habitable for prolonged periods of time.[7]

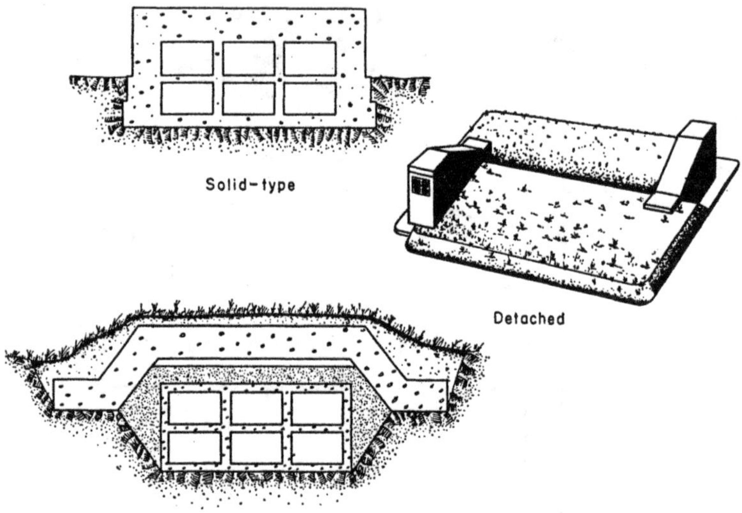

FIG. 9. Heavy air-raid shelters.

Heavy detached shelters with very thick walls and roofs of reinforced concrete are similar to World War II bunkers, with some types built only partly below ground level (see fig. 9).[8] They would seem to be designed to withstand from 200 to 300 psi and, like the deep shelters, are equipped to allow long-term occupancy.[9]

Soviet manuals suggest that these shelters will not be available to the population on a large scale; in all likelihood they are intended for select government, Party, military, and civil defense personnel.

PLATE 1. View of a Moscow subway station

Plate 2. View of an entrance to a Moscow subway station indicating a concealed door in the floor

PLATE 3. View of an entrance to a Moscow subway station indicating a concealed door in the wall

Detached Shelters

A current civil defense manual states:

> In cities with a large population there are special structures in which several thousand persons can take shelter simultaneously. These shelters offer the highest degree of protection. This type of structure includes underground shelters as well as ferroconcrete shelters partly buried in the ground with sufficiently thick roofs and walls. Their protective covering is designed in such a way that they are capable of surviving not only the impact of the shock wave of an atomic explosion, but also a direct hit by a high-explosive bomb.[10]

In practice, of course, shelter capacities depend on their location and purpose: there are shelters designed to accommodate only about 150 persons, whereas those intended as industrial or public facilities may have space for several thousand people.[11]

Most detached shelters are below ground level and are built of reinforced concrete that is covered by a mound of earth several feet thick.[12] The concrete roof is supported by pillars and by walls, which divide the shelter into compartments for greater strength and as a safeguard for the occupants in case of partial damage (see figs. 10 and 11). Structures of this type appear to have a blast resistance of 100–150 psi.[13] The two or more entrances will be provided with steel doors and air locks. Filter ventilation units, heating, water, toilets, and communication equipment form part of the standard provisions, and there may also be power generators or batteries, chemical air purifiers, bottled oxygen, and stocks of food.[14]

Subways

The manuals clearly indicate that cities with subways will use these as public shelters in time of war.[15] First Deputy Premier F. Kozlov confirmed this intention during his visit to New York, in 1959, when he advised New York Governor Rockefeller not to try to build shelters under every building, but to put the

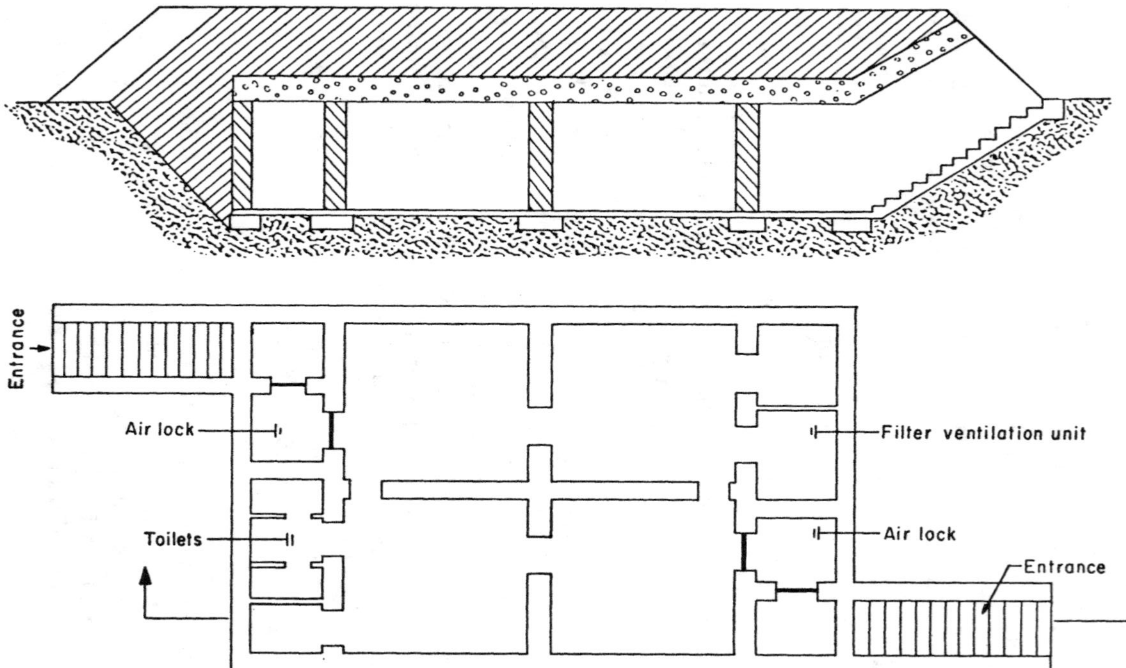

FIG. 10. Detached shelter.

money into subways: "Why don't you build subways like we have—good subways and deep subways. You could improve your subways and provide bomb shelters at the same time."[16] And a Soviet civil defense manual stresses the effectiveness of subways as shelters: "Special underground structures (of the

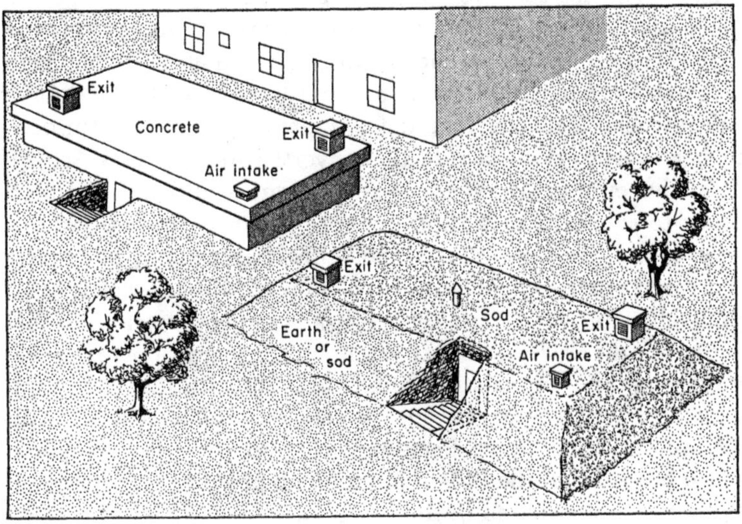

Fig. 11. Detached shelters.

subway type) are distinguished by their specially high protective quality, and in their ability to withstand an atomic explosion they are superior to all other types of shelters."[17]

A number of Soviet cities now have subway systems. The oldest, in Moscow, on which construction began in 1931, served as an air-raid shelter for hundreds of thousands of Moscovites during World War II. Its present length is about 43 miles, not counting a 2-mile-long tunnel in the center of the city which has not been used since its completion in 1953.[18] Under the current Seven Year Plan, it is intended to expand the subway system by 35 miles and to add forty stations to the fifty-six now in operation.[19] The Moscow subway is double-tracked, with each track laid in a separate, tubular, concrete-lined tunnel. Most of the station platforms and tunnels, which are reached by a system of escalators, are very deep—in fact, deeper than might seem necessary for purely technical reasons—with some more than 120 feet below street level.[20] In the event of a nuclear explosion, the stations and platforms themselves, being very large and ornate, could be dangerous because of flying debris, but it seems clear from civil defense manuals that track tunnels, rather than stations, are to be converted into shelters (see pl. 1).[21] The present Moscow subway system would have enough space to shelter one million or more persons, or about 20 per cent of the city's population, and this capacity may be greatly increased when the present expansion of the subway is completed.[22] The *New York Times* has commented on a double tunnel in the center of the city as having "no transport purpose, merely paralleling existing lines," and constituting "undoubtedly the world's largest and safest air-raid shelter."[23] And Khrushchev may have been referring to the subway system when he said that the largest atom-bomb-proof shelter system in the world was situated in the center of Moscow.[24]

The Leningrad subway, built only in the postwar years, is similar in construction to the Moscow system. With about 8 miles of track already in operation, it is still being expanded. As of now, it could quite possibly shelter about 200,000 persons in its stations and tunnels.[25]

In November, 1960, the first section of a subway system was put into operation in Kiev. At present, 6.25 miles of track, with eight stations, are in use, and there are plans for further expansion.[26] Although similar to the Moscow subway, the Kiev system may be even deeper, and conceivably could shelter as many as 200,000 persons, or 18 per cent of the city's population.

Even though the Moscow subway furnished effective shelter during World War II, ordinary subways would not provide adequate protection against atomic weapons. Depth and strength of construction alone would not suffice in a nuclear war. To be fully effective shelters, the subways would have to be sealed against blast, fallout, and chemical and bacteriological agents, and equipped for long-term occupancy. The Soviet press has given no indication whether any of the subway systems have been adapted for these purposes. However, there is evidence that the subways have been provided with concealed doors at the entrances to the train platforms (see pls. 2 and 3.[27] At the same time, it should be noted that Soviet subways do not normally have public toilets and running water. If such facilities have been installed, they are likely to be situated in the tunnels rather than in the stations, since the former will be the main shelters in the event of an attack.

We do not know to what extent railroad, vehicular, and pedestrian tunnels have been adapted for use as shelters, though the desirability of doing so is mentioned in the manuals. Nor is there any indication of how many such underground passages exist in Soviet cities, and thus of the number of persons they could accommodate if converted into shelters.

Basement Shelters

It is said in the Soviet Union that one of the more widely available collective means of protection are the shelters built into the basements of multistory apartment houses, and industrial, school, and public buildings.[28] According to a civil defense handbook, they are

> . . . simple and at the same time reliable means of defense. They protect [the population] from the effects of an atomic bomb explosion (at some distance from the center of the explosion), from the effects of the blast wave and of splinters resulting from the explosion of high-explosive and fragmentation bombs near the shelter, from toxic and radioactive matter, and other known means of destruction.
>
> These shelters are located in the basement part of buildings, which is very convenient for those who seek shelter. People can rapidly descend into such shelters at any time of the day when the air alert is sounded.[29]

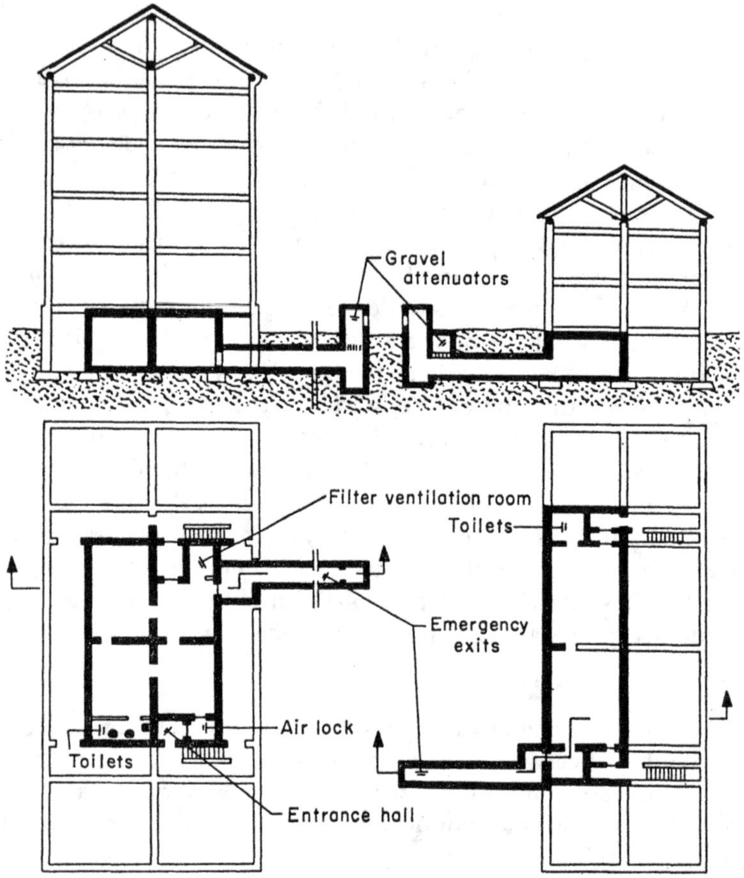

FIG. 12. Basement shelter.

The typical Soviet basement shelter is thus more than merely a cover against fallout. It is customarily designed to provide space for 100 to 300 persons, 150 being the recommended capacity.[30] Usually, it will occupy only a part of the basement. Ideally, the shelter will be in the center, so as to take advantage of the double shield provided by the external walls of the basement (see fig. 12).[31] If this is not possible, the shelter has to use one or more of the building walls. Entirely below ground, the basement shelter must have a roof of reinforced concrete strong enough to withstand the blast wave of an atomic bomb "at some distance" from the explosion or a direct hit on the building by a high-explosive bomb, and if the building collapses, it must be able to bear the weight of the debris.[32] Furthermore, the roof has to be fireproof and sufficiently insulated to shield the shelter occupants from the heat of large fires. The walls of the shelter may be made either of reinforced concrete or of several thicknesses of brick. For added strength and safety, the shelter is compartmented by a number of bearing walls of concrete or brick, and the roof is further supported by steel or ferroconcrete beams or plates.[33] Depending on the construction material used and the thickness of the roofs and walls, the basement shelter is designed to withstand a blast pressure of 10–100 psi.[34] Most of them are likely to be built to survive in the lower range of blast pressure.

To render them proof against radioactive, chemical, and bacteriological agents, the entrances to the basement shelter are each protected by double steel doors of the bulkhead type, which are edged with rubber to make them fully airtight.[35] The filter ventilation unit is located in a separate room inside the shelter to avoid endangering the occupants if it becomes contaminated by radioactive or toxic agents.[36] Some shelters have an exhaust system as well. The required emergency exit (see fig. 13) consists of a tunnel, about half as long as the building is high, which usually terminates in a concrete block above ground, with one or more openings covered by louvered doors or plates; occasionally, the tunnel merely leads into a manhole.[37] According to the manuals, all exits are equipped with gravel blast attenuators. Basement shelters in adjoining buildings may be connected by underground passages, which also serve as emergency exits. The exits are usually in the backyards of the buildings or in adjoining gardens.[38]

For long-term occupancy the shelters are equipped with water, toilets, special containers for drinking water, heat, electric light and power, storage batteries, double-decker bunks, telephones, radio receivers, medical supplies, and fire-fighting and digging apparatus, and they may also be provided with bottled oxygen.[39]

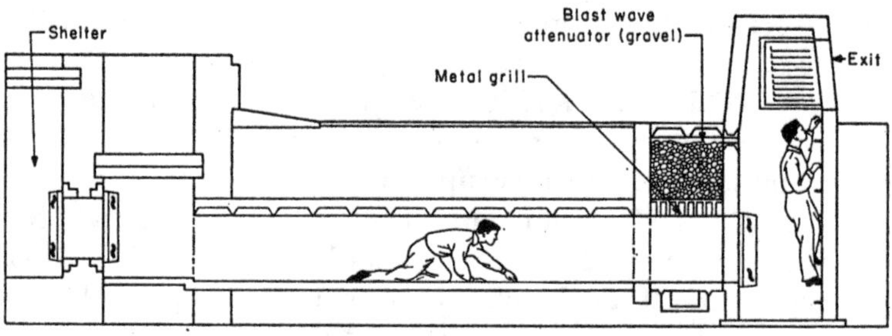

FIG. 13. Shelter emergency exit.

The type of basement shelter described here is usually mentioned in connection with new construction, rather than with respect to buildings erected before World War II. Little is said about adapting these older basements, or World War II shelters, to modern requirements. The Soviets admit that the older facilities, which were adequate protection against conventional weapons, would not be effective against nuclear weapons.

Civil defense publications do state that some older basements with particularly strong cover—especially vaulted roofs—lend themselves to being turned into shelters.[40] It is said also that basements with strong roofs can be reinforced and made fireproof, and that window wells may be filled and sealed. One recommendation is to strengthen the roof with reinforced concrete slabs resting on steel beams and supported by concrete, brick, or wooden supports (see fig. 14).[41] To improve the shelter's fire and heat resistance, and as an additional shield against radiation, the roof may be covered with a foot-deep layer of sand.[42] An emergency escape tunnel and exit would have to be

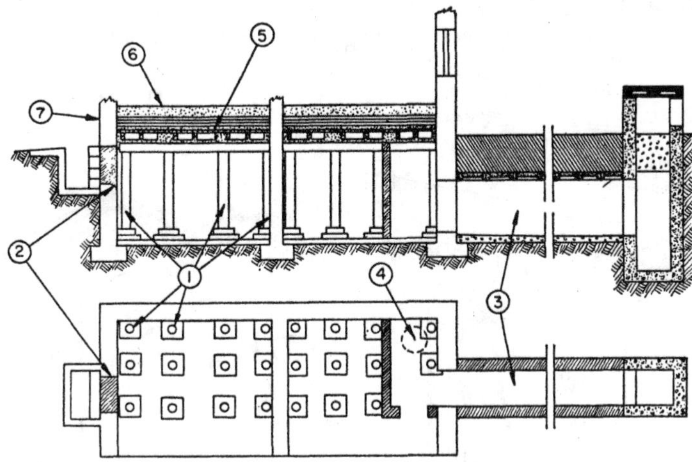

① Posts (dia = 20 cm)
② Covered windows
③ Emergency tunnel
④ Filter-ventilation unit
⑤ Wooden boards to guard against splinters
⑥ Layer of earth (30 cm) to reduce instant radiation
⑦ Concrete slab

FIG. 14. Adaptation of a cellar to serve as a shelter.

added, and blast and sealing doors, filter ventilation facilities, and other essential equipment would need to be installed.

Suburban Family Shelters

Although family shelters do not appear to constitute an important part of the Soviet shelter program, they are occasionally referred to as being suitable for the use of suburban residents. According to one article, residents of one- or two-family houses in the suburbs may, at their own expense, build shelters that will protect them against some blast, as well as against heat and radiation.[43] Either permanent or emergency shelters are suggested: the former, to be built in peacetime of metal sheeting or concrete (see fig. 15); the latter, to be made of wood or other light material (see fig. 16) only at the acute threat of war. Either type must be several feet below ground level to benefit from the

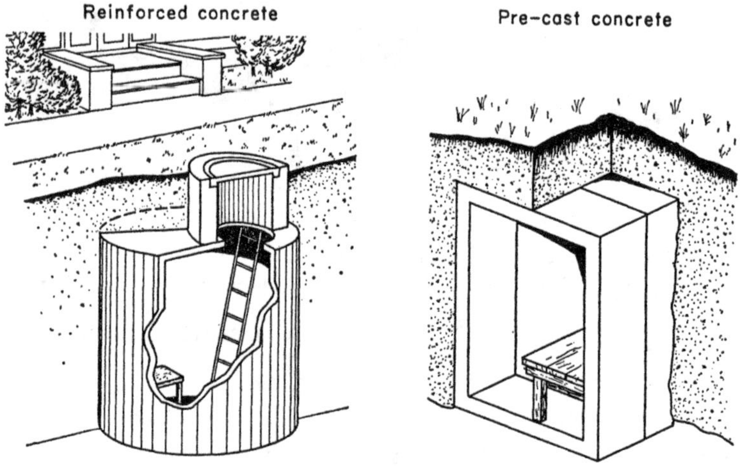

FIG. 15. Suburban one-family shelters.

shielding effect of the earth, and will be some distance away from the building. Among various possible designs the one especially recommended is a pipe of reinforced concrete about 6 feet in diameter.[44] These private shelters should provide from 5 to 10 square feet of space per person, and be equipped with doors and simple filter-ventilation units.

In view of the scant attention they receive in Soviet civil defense literature, family shelters are unlikely to be given much prominence in the over-all shelter program. Moreover, individual families would find the procurement of building material, labor, and financing for such private construction fraught with many difficulties and obstacles, not to mention that a Soviet homeowner may be dispossessed without compensation if the city authorities decide to use the area of his property for other kinds of construction. As family shelters are entirely voluntary ventures, few persons are likely to have the necessary money and influence to build them. Conceivably, this

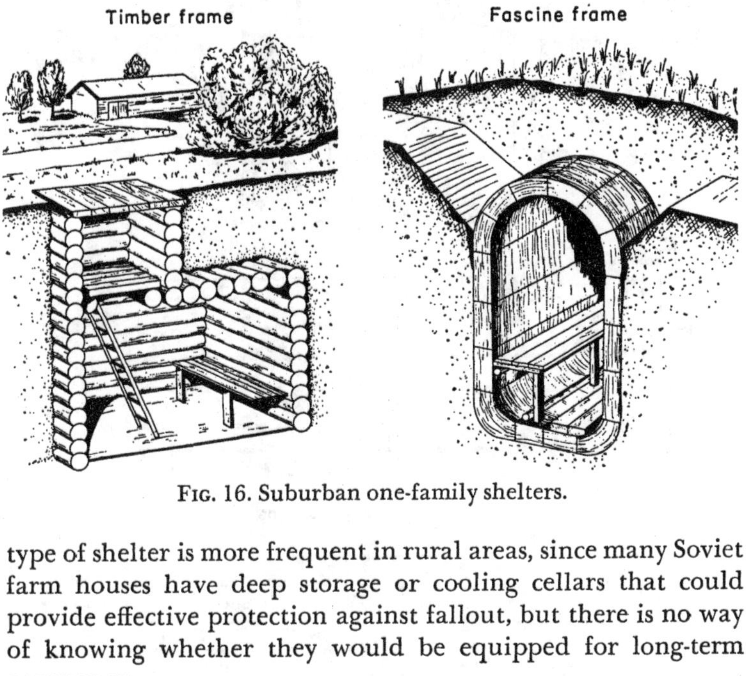

FIG. 16. Suburban one-family shelters.

type of shelter is more frequent in rural areas, since many Soviet farm houses have deep storage or cooling cellars that could provide effective protection against fallout, but there is no way of knowing whether they would be equipped for long-term occupancy.

Emergency Shelters

In addition to the permanent shelters in cities and at important industrial and strategic sites, several types of emergency shelters are to be built as soon as the Soviet government believes there is danger of a war. In the cities, these shelters will supple-

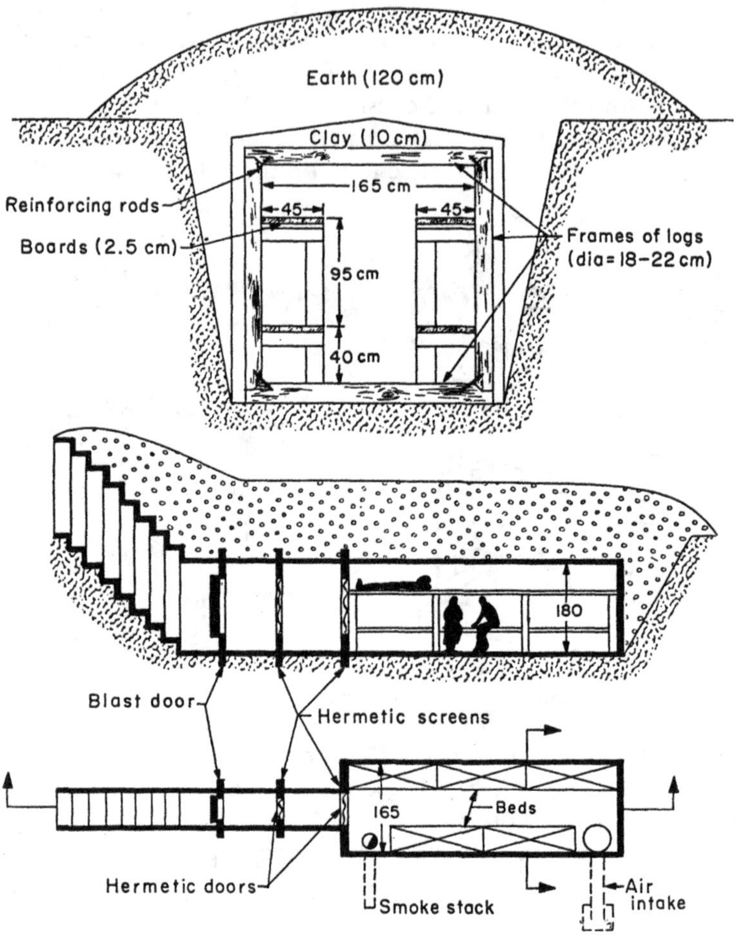

FIG. 17. Dugout shelter.

ment the permanent facilities; in rural areas, they will provide the main protection.[45]

The two most elaborate of the various types of emergency shelters described in the manuals are dugouts and galleries in hillsides (see figs. 17 and 18). Both may be built either in peacetime or at short notice. The typical dugout is described as an underground room lined with 6-inch slabs of precast concrete or timber, with a blast door and several gasproof sealing doors.[46] For waterproofing, it is covered with 4–10 inches of compacted clay topped by 3–4 feet of earth. Dugouts are designed for relatively long-term occupancy, and may be equipped with heating, bucket toilets, simple filter ventilation units, water containers, batteries, and double-decker bunks. The average dugout is about 5 feet wide and can accommodate 30 or more persons.[47] Such a shelter will provide adequate protection against direct and fallout radiation, heat, and falling debris. Concrete-lined dugouts have considerable blast resistance and are said to be able to survive in the zone of medium destruction of a nuclear explosion.[48]

Galleries consist either of a single tunnel built into a hillside or of two parallel tunnels connected by a third tunnel deep under the hill. The hill itself provides a considerable earth cover. The tunnels, framed with timber or precast concrete slabs, are 4–5 feet wide and 6–7 feet high.[49] The single tunnel can shelter about 20 persons, and the double-tunnel system is designed for 60 persons or more.[50] The entrance is protected by a shielding wall and a concrete-slab roof. A gallery shelter may have heating facilities, simple filter ventilation units, toilets, and double-decker bunks.

The simpler emergency shelters, which provide less protection against blast and no protection at all against chemical and bacteriological agents, are not suitable for long-term occupancy.[51] Most of them are covered zigzag trenches, framed with timber, sheet metal, precast concrete slabs, or any other material that is handy (see fig. 19), and covered with 2–4 feet of earth and a waterproof layer of compacted clay.[52] Another type consists of a ferroconcrete pipe, 6 feet in diameter, 3–8 inches thick, and buried under 3 feet of earth.[53] Depending on their length, these simple shelters can accommodate from 20 to 60 persons. How-

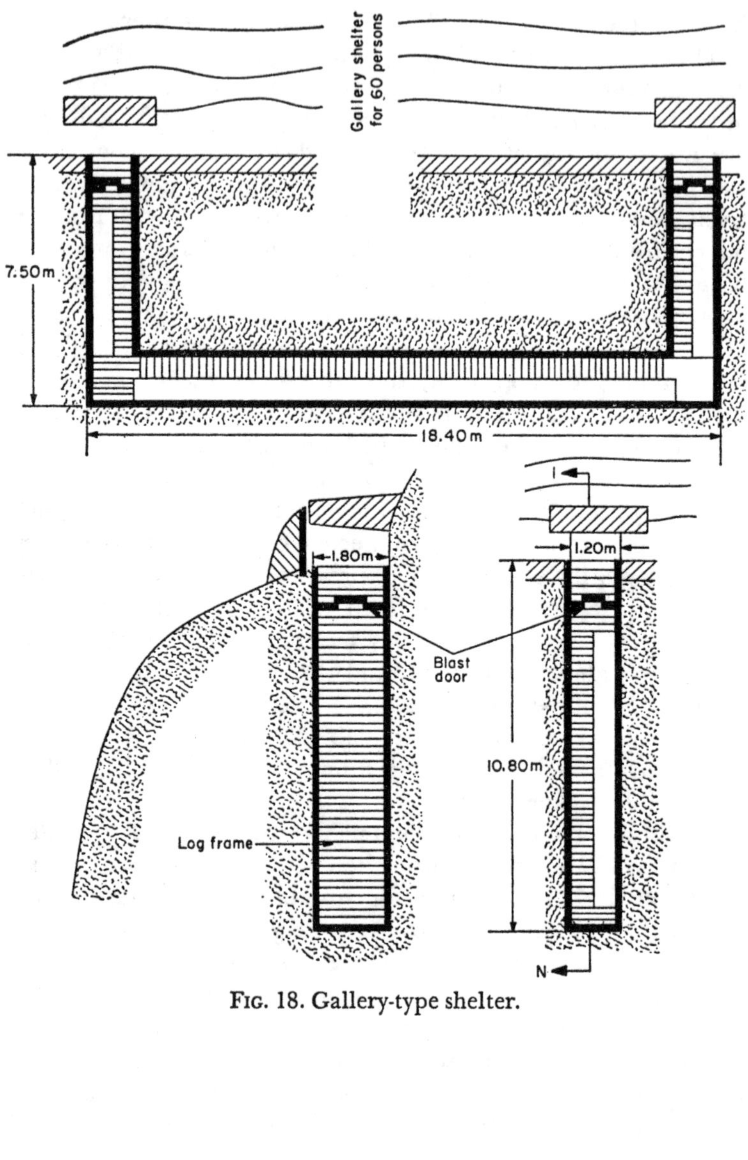

Fig. 18. Gallery-type shelter.

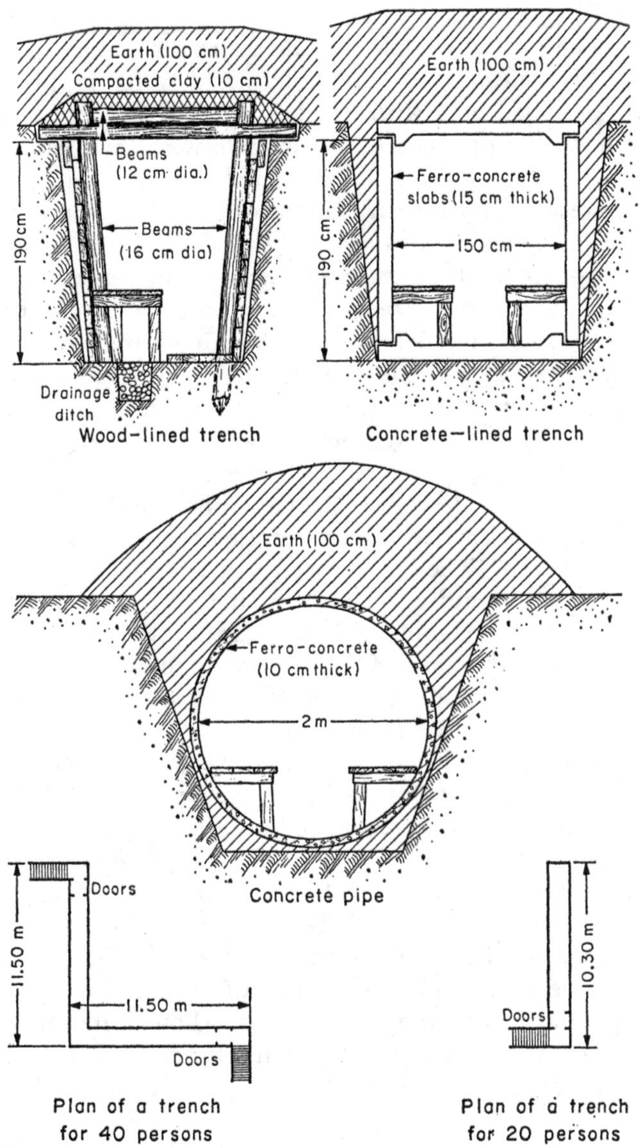

FIG. 19. Covered trenches.

ever, in their basic layout, they lack airtight sealing or blast doors, filter ventilation units, toilets, and water supply, and will be provided only with benches. As these shelters are not gasproof, the occupants are instructed to wear their gas masks during an attack.[54] Such shelters could provide adequate protection in areas of low-intensity fallout, where there would be no need for prolonged occupancy.

The simpler kinds of emergency shelters supposedly can be built very quickly, since their sites have been surveyed in peacetime by the local civil defense units, which are trained to mark the construction of these shelters in a matter of minutes.[55] Actual construction is to begin only at the "threatening situation" alert, one of the civil defense warning signals, which is sounded when the government believes war to be an acute possibility.[56] The citizens will thereupon be mobilized to build these emergency shelters under the supervision of local civil defense personnel. The actual construction of a 60-man covered trench is said to require 200–250 man-hours of work, and thus, supposedly, can be completed in one day or less if the necessary building material is at hand.[57] According to this claim, it would take the authorities only a few days to provide most, if not all, of the people with some form of shelter.

Recent Soviet civil defense literature also recommends the construction of shelters for valuable large farm animals.[58] These would protect the cattle against fallout, heat, and to some extent against blast. Built entirely below ground level, they will be framed with timber covered by several feet of earth. Farm workers in charge of the animals are to be provided with shelters nearby. As noted above, many villages and collective farms already have ready-made underground facilities in the form of cooling cellars and storage basements, whose suitability and adaptability for use as emergency fallout shelters is mentioned in Soviet manuals.[59]

Shelter Habitability

Full protection against the effects of nuclear, chemical, or bacteriological attack may require a long stay in the shelter, the exact length of time depending on the intensity and nature of the contamination, the speed with which natural decay will reduce it to a safe level, and the extent of the decontamination work possible. The need for shelter occupancy may therefore vary from a few days to several months. (In the United States, the longest time assumed likely to be necessary for fallout radiation to decline to a safe level is two weeks.) Whether people can actually remain under cover for as long as is necessary will depend on the type of shelter, its equipment, facilities, and supplies, and on the behavior of the occupants. There must be sufficient space per person, filtered air, water, food, toilets, and other essential facilities.

Just how quickly people can reach cover will depend, of course, on the number of shelters available and on their location. Ideally, there should be shelters both at a person's place of work and at his residence, as well as sufficient other scattered shelter facilities to permit every urban resident to reach cover within 15–20 minutes after the first sounding of the air-raid warning. (The number and accessibility of shelters in the Soviet Union is discussed below.)

Most shelters have several entrances, which should be adequate to permit the rapid entry of the 100 to 300 people for which the average shelter is designed. Basement shelters in apartment houses appear to be easily accessible to the residents. The newer Soviet apartment buildings are usually five to seven stories high, with four apartments to each floor.[60] There are no elevators, and only a single staircase leads from the top floor to the basement. Most buildings have no fire-escapes, on the grounds that they are made of fire-resistant material and the existing staircases are sufficient for rapid evacuation. In view

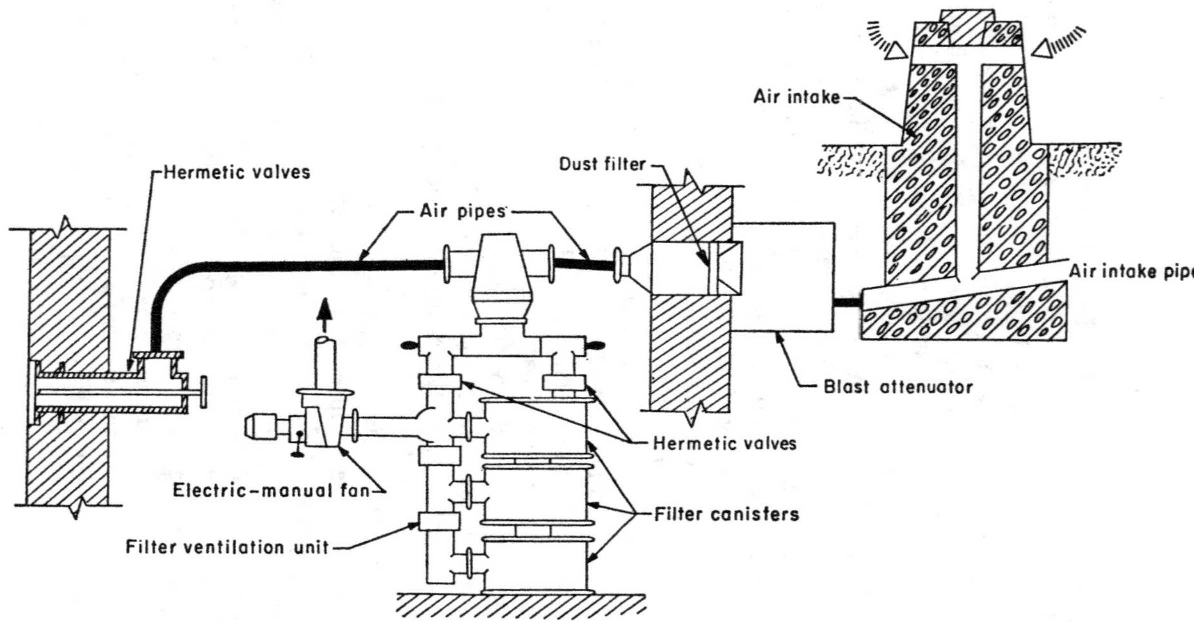

Fig. 20. Filter ventilation unit.

of the relatively small number of apartments in a typical building, the residents could probably reach the basement shelter within 10–15 minutes after the sounding of the alert.

Subway shelters present a more difficult problem from the viewpoints of speedy access and full utilization. In the center of Moscow, the subway stations are sufficiently numerous so that any person in that area could reach a station in 20 minutes or less. Outside the center, however, the stations are more widely separated. Although the three or four escalators that are the rule in most stations will allow a fairly rapid descent to the lower platforms, it will take much longer to move people into and through the tunnels that are to be the actual shelters.

The amount of floor space the average citizen is likely to find inside a public shelter is only 5–10 square feet per occupant, with ceilings of 8–10 feet in the permanent, and 6–8 feet in temporary shelters.[61] The double-decker bunks will be 18 inches wide, and only the top ones will be used for sleeping, while the bottom bunks will serve as seats.[62] Thus, the occupants would have to take turns lying down. The simpler emergency shelters are to have nothing but benches, and the subways, according to the illustrations in civil defense manuals, will have neither seating nor sleeping facilities except for makeshift boards or wooden platforms covering the tracks.[63] In short, a prolonged stay in any Soviet shelter is likely to be uncomfortable. On the other hand, the citizens are more used to crowded conditions than are their Western counterparts and thus might not find it unbearable. It is possible that shelters for the elite will have more space and better facilities.

The supply of fresh air is to be assured by a rather complex but effective filter ventilation unit, which has been standardized for many years. The unit, known as model FVA-49, is electrically or hand-operated and consists of an air intake, a blast-attenuator, a dust filter, and three chemical canister filters (see fig. 20).[64] From the intake, the air passes through a blast-attenuator situated outside the shelter which consists of a layer of 24–31 inches of gravel (see fig. 21).[65] Next, it passes through the dust filter (a mesh covered with an oily substance), also situated outside the shelter, which will filter out fallout as well as dust.[66] Thereafter, the air reënters the shelter, to be distributed either

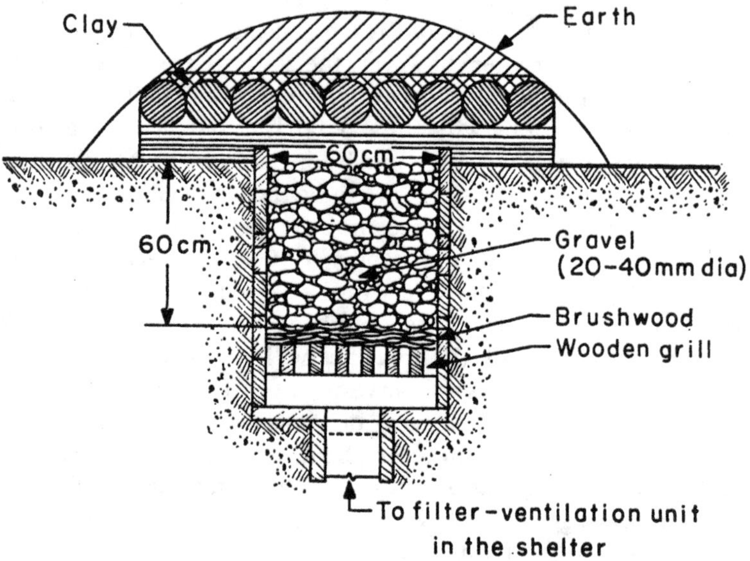

FIG. 21. Simple gravel blast-attenuator.

directly or by way of three chemical-mechanical filter canisters that can trap chemical and bacteriological agents.[67] (An emergency air intake goes into operation if the main intake is damaged.) This sizable unit is about 6 feet high and 3.5 feet wide, with each filter canister alone about 16.5 inches high and 20 inches in diameter. Special indicators attached to the canisters show the presence of certain chemical agents and the extent to which they are being absorbed.[68] There is a gauge showing the amount of air flowing into the shelter, and also an air-pressure gauge. During an attack, a special valve will seal off the unit to reduce the possibility of its being damaged by blast. A standard filter ventilation unit is capable of filtering 2 cubic meters of air per hour or 1.177 cubic feet per minute per person in a 150-man shelter.[69] This throughput appears to be adequate to keep the carbon dioxide concentration within physiologically tolerable limits, especially if the shelter air can be supplemented with some bottled oxygen.

To prevent contaminated air from seeping into the shelter through tiny fissures, the air pressure in the shelter is maintained at a level somewhat higher (5 millimeters on a water-air-pressure reading set) than the air pressure outside.[70] This process is regulated by means of an exhaust valve that closes automatically.

One shortcoming of this ventilation system is the absence of temperature and humidity controls. There is no cooling system. Temperature and humidity in a tightly packed shelter are bound to rise rapidly, and might become unbearable within a few days. The amount of air supplied by filter ventilation, while sufficient for normal breathing, might not be enough to cool the shelter and carry off the heat. This problem would be further aggravated if the outside air that was being drawn into the shelter were hot, either naturally or as a result of fires. Of course, if no chemical and bacteriological agents were present, it would not be necessary to use the chemical filters, and once the fallout had settled, it might then be safe to open the shelter doors for ventilation. Large public shelters may in fact have more elaborate filter ventilation systems, equipped with temperature and humidity control devices, than the one described here, which is primarily designed for basement shelters.

Stocking shelters with water, and especially with enough food, for extended occupancy is bound to constitute a difficult problem in the Soviet Union. Apparently, the civil defense authorities have not developed any special shelter rations. Food could conceivably be stored in advance in certain special shelters, such as the deep or detached shelters that are operated by governmental or industrial agencies (fig. 8 shows food-storage space in a deep shelter), but this is not practicable in apartment house shelters. For one reason, Soviet citizens, who make far less use of canned food and refrigeration than do Westerners, do not store much food at home. For another, any food stocks not under guard would be in danger of being stolen. Moreover, basement shelters are kept locked in peacetime, and a tenant who stored his provisions there would not have free access to them. Consequently all persons using public, basement, or emergency shelters are instructed at present to prepare food packages for "several" days as soon as the "threatening situation" alert is sounded, and to take these with them into the shelter or wherever else they may go after the alert.[71]

The average citizen will probably not have more than a three-day supply of food with him at the time he takes cover. Before leaving their homes, however, people are instructed to protect against contamination whatever supplies they must leave behind. According to manuals, therefore, they may be able, in areas of low fallout, to obtain additional provisions from their apartments fairly soon after an attack.[72] Nevertheless, the time that people could count on spending in apartment-house or emergency shelters is obviously limited by the amount of food they were able to bring in.

Arrangements for the provision of water in the Soviet shelters are somewhat better than the plans for providing food. As many of them as possible are supplied with running water from the city's water system or from wells.[73] This water will be used primarily for washing, and most sketches of typical basement shelters show that there will be two washbasins, but no showers. For drinking, it appears, special containers of boiled or safe water are to be kept in every shelter.[74] In addition, people are instructed to bring a supply of drinking water to the shelter along with their food.[75] In time of danger the population will also store water in their homes in covered containers and bathtubs. But even though water may be somewhat more plentiful than food in most basement shelters, it would probably not suffice for a long stay, especially if temperature and humidity were high or if the city's water system were destroyed.

The shelters do not seem to be well equipped with toilet facilities. Most shelter designs show only two such facilities for 100 to 150 persons.

Control inside the shelter will be the task of the civil defense shelter team, aided by members of other teams. They will be responsible for opening and closing shelter doors, operating the filter ventilation system and other equipment, and maintaining order among the occupants.[76] The people themselves, as part of their civil defense training, will also have been taught how to operate the equipment and how to behave in a shelter (no smoking, no unnecessary movement, no eating without permission, and so forth).[77]

No one may leave a shelter without the permission of the shelter commander. In the event of a nuclear attack, this would normally not be granted until a civil defense reconnaissance of the area has determined that it is safe for people to come out. Otherwise, the shelter commander will order the shelter cleared only if he is instructed to do so by civil defense rescue units, if the shelter is damaged, or if its occupants are threatened by fire, flooding, or other hazards.[78]

It is obvious from the facilities described here that the Soviet authorities are not planning in terms of prolonged occupancy of basement and emergency shelters, and this is freely admitted in the civil defense literature, as in this passage from an article: "In some districts, where contamination is especially high, it may not decline to a safe level for a long time—in some instances, for many weeks. Naturally, it is not possible for people to remain in shelters and cover for so long a period."[79] As we shall see, Soviet operational doctrine has taken this fact into consideration.

It is impossible to determine just how many Soviet shelters are kept ready for instant use, since a number of them seem to be used in peacetime for "cultural" or other purposes.[80] According to one manual, for instance: "All shelters used for cultural or practical purposes are immediately cleared and prepared for their primary purpose as soon as the 'threatening situation' alert is announced. Control over the carrying-out of these measures is exercised by the local civil defense staff of the city or borough."[81] There is no reason to assume, however, that this statement affects many of the existing shelters.

Shelter Availability

Neither the manuals nor the Soviet press reveal anything of the scope of the shelter construction program or the amount of shelter space already available. Most tourists in the Soviet Union fail to notice any evidence of the existence of shelters. Mikoyan's statement in Cleveland, on January 7, 1959, would seem to be part of a deliberate Soviet attempt to reinforce the impression abroad that the USSR is still without shelters and has no serious intention of embarking on a shelter program. He said: "Our scientists are trying to find out the means of building shelters or otherwise to save people from these bombs, but when one has knowledge of what the bomb really is, one thinks that all these shelters are merely a matter of consolation until the bomb has exploded, because there is no defense against the bomb."[82] Significantly, this passage was deleted from the report of Mikoyan's speech published in *Pravda,* as was also Mrs. Kruschev's similar statement of October 6, 1961.

These statements, the failure of many travelers to detect shelters, and the lack of published Soviet statistics on the subject do not, however, constitute evidence against the existence of an active and extensive shelter construction program. The dearth of published information in this area is in keeping with the secrecy surrounding so many Soviet activities; it does not necessarily bespeak a lack of interest in civil defense. If travelers fail to observe existing shelter facilities, it is because they are unfamiliar with Soviet shelter characteristics, because they are on a restricted, guided tour and do not speak Russian, and because as a matter of policy the Soviet authorities do not plan to put up signs indicating the location of shelters until the "threatening situation" alert.[83] In the meantime, the citizen learns, as a part of his civil defense training, the location of shelters nearest to his place of work and his residence.[84] Mikoyan's statement must be regarded as primarily part of the general emphasis on the destructiveness of a thermonuclear war in the propagandistic attempt to deter the United States from resorting to war in defense of its interests. Not only is his statement contradicted by the remarks of First Deputy Premier Kozlov that were quoted earlier, but there are other indications that the Soviet authorities have made, and continue to make, considerable investments in shelter construction, far greater than could be explained as merely a gesture for the people's "peace of mind." There can be little doubt that the government believes in the worth of shelters. Admittedly, most types of Soviet shelters could not survive at the point of a nuclear explosion (which would probably cover about 0.3 per cent of the total area of destruction); but Soviet and satellite assessments of the value of different shelters indicate that most of them will be adequate in the zones of medium and light damage (which may account for more than 80 per cent of the total area of destruction), and will provide full protection against fallout and chemical and bacteriological agents.[85]

Scant though they are, the indications in the Soviet press pointing to actual shelter construction are all the more significant in view of the general policy of not publicizing these activities. There is evidence, for example, that the civil defense authorities have had a say in approving construction plans for new buildings at least as far back as 1941, and that these plans have incorporated civil defense features. According to the following statement, published in 1941, "Architects and builders of civil construction are obliged to take into account the requirements of air defense in every house that is built and to come to an agreement with the local civil defense staff concerning the measures to be taken in this field."[86] New factory and housing construction plans were to meet "the requirements of civil defense," which were "set out in special instructions."[87] In 1946, a resolution of the Stalingrad civil defense authorities announced: "We succeeded in arranging it so that not a single building plan will be approved by the expert commission without the consent of the city civil defense."[88] For Stalingrad, this undoubtedly meant incorporating civil defense features in many of the city's structures, which had been largely destroyed during the war and were now being rebuilt.

The practice of requiring civil defense approval of building plans continued at least until 1958, when a book that regularly lists all approving agencies failed for the first time to include the civil defense authorities.[89]

It is of course entirely possible that civil defense control nevertheless continued into the present, as is implied in civil defense manuals published after 1958.[90] But whether or not the inclusion of civil defense features has now ceased to be obligatory, the above quotations would seem to indicate that for the first ten years or more of postwar factory and apartment-house building, it was an essential part of the program. Even if the requirement of civil defense approval was not always enforced strictly, it is likely over the years to have resulted in the construction of substantial numbers of shelters.

Other evidence of the existence and growing number of shelters may be found in the civil defense training programs. Whereas the earlier training courses were largely theoretical, the last two have insisted on practical work involving the use of shelters. Instructors today are directed to conduct their classes on "collective means of defense" in existing shelters, to teach everyone how to operate shelter equipment, to acquaint each trainee with the shelters nearest his place of work and residence, to teach the proper use of emergency exits, and so on.[91] There is additional evidence, in the Soviet press, that training actually does take place in shelters.[92] Further confirmation may be found in the occasional mentions and descriptions of shelters in the newspapers, including for example, a published photograph of the filter ventilation system in the "Tashkabel" factory shelter in Tashkent (Uzbek SSR),[93] and the reports of shelters in a Moscow petroleum plant and in a weaving plant in Minsk.[94] The press also makes incidental reference to basement shelters in Moscow, Riga (Latvian SSR), Zhdanov (Ukrainian SSR), Rostov/Don, Makeevka (Ukrainian SSR), Leningrad, Stalingrad, Elektrostal, Simferopol, and also on several collective farms.[95] Some travelers have observed shelters in such cities as Moscow, Leningrad, Kursk, Kiev, Stalingrad, Baku, Tbilisi, and Tashkent. It is significant that this list of localities spreads over an area stretching from the Baltic Sea to Central Asia and from the Gulf of Finland to the Black Sea, and that it includes cities of such varying size and importance. It may be assumed that shelters, other than subways, could be found in many Soviet cities for which the newspapers thus far have supplied no corroboration.

The total Soviet shelter capacity certainly cannot be assessed from public sources. In Moscow, it probably exceeds 20 per cent of the residents, since at least that number could find space in the subway alone, and the press mentions additional shelters in factories and apartment houses. According to the afore-mentioned testimony by Mr. Ellis, a "secret report indicated that the Soviet Union was building enough shelters to protect the great majority of its population from fallout in the event of nuclear war."[96] Despite our lack of conclusive information on the precise scope of the program, there can be no doubt that ever since World War II the Soviet authorities have been seriously engaged in a shelter construction program designed to provide some degree of protection for possibly a majority of the urban population. Civil defense planners obviously have no thought of being able to protect such vast numbers against all the effects of nuclear weapons, and appear to be reserving the better facilities for select administrative, Party, industrial, and military elements. Also, they may be losing some of their earlier confidence in the effectiveness of basement shelters in view of the growing yield of thermonuclear weapons. But present indications are that the planners have not abandoned the over-all program of shelter construction. Conceivably, their future efforts will be directed toward providing more and better blast protection and enabling a greater number of people to remain in their shelters for protracted periods of time.

7

Evacuation

Before 1958, Soviet civil defense manuals, apparently satisfied that shelters were sufficient to protect urban residents, never mentioned the possibility of evacuation. Since then, however, the civil defense authorities have openly turned their attention to urban evacuation as a part of the defense plan. Significantly, this has also been the period of their growing recognition of the destructiveness of thermonuclear weapons.

The earlier reluctance to plan the large-scale evacuation of cities may have stemmed, in part, from the serious difficulties of production, transportation, feeding, and quartering that the authorities had experienced in evacuations during the war. In 1958, however, there were signs of a definite change in Soviet civil defense doctrine on this point. A civil defense manual published in June of that year mentioned for the first time the creation of a Transport Service, which would ensure the "evacuation from cities of institutions (nurseries, schools, kindergartens, etc.), of elements of the population unfit for work, [and] of persons wounded as a result of an air attack."[1] The Service for Maintaining Public Order and Safety would coöperate with the Transport Service in safeguarding "the evacuation of elements of the population unfit for work."[2]

The basic Soviet civil defense handbook, also published in 1958, was still more explicit. It characterized as one of the essential duties of the MPVO the "institution of measures for the dispersal (evacuation) of the population . . . ,"[3] and stated that "evacuating the people in time, especially from large cities, will significantly reduce the number of casualties. . . ."[4] At that time, however, civil defense instructors were told nothing about the organization and operation of a possible evacuation, perhaps because the newly created Transport Service had not yet worked out the necessary plans.

An article on rural civil defense measures published at the end of 1958 is the first indication of a developing plan: "When the 'threatening situation' alert is sounded, rural areas will organize . . . the reception and quartering of, and work arrangements for, the urban population evacuated to the countryside."[5] Another article says that if time permitted it would be desirable for city residents, upon hearing the air-raid alert, to walk out beyond the city limits because "in the suburban area the likelihood of casualties from debris is less great, and at the same time there are, as a rule, more places that could provide cover than in the cities. . . ."[6]

Since these first, somewhat general statements, the authorities appear to have developed more specific evacuation plans and operational concepts. The new handbook for public instructors teaching the 18-hour training course contains three pages of discussion of evacuation (calling it "one of the most important measures instituted for the purpose of protecting the population"), and stipulates that of the first 50 minutes of instruction, 15 are to be devoted to this subject.[7] Still more details were published in 1960 in a special article on the organization and procedures of evacuation.[8]

The evacuation of urban residents is the responsibility of the executive committees of the city soviets, which organize (now—

in peacetime) permanent evacuation commissions at the city and borough levels.[9] These commissions work in conjunction with the Transport Service, the Service for Maintaining Public Order and Safety, and the Medical Service. The manuals distinguish among three stages and kinds of evacuation: (1) pre-attack evacuation, (2) evacuation while the country is under attack, and (3) post-attack evacuation of survivors from highly contaminated areas.

Pre-attack evacuation begins with the "threatening situation" alert.[10] At that time, the radio or press will announce the categories of residents subject to compulsory evacuation, the order in which evacuation is to proceed, and such details as assembly points, amount of authorized baggage, and the location of persons in charge.[11] First to be evacuated will be those in orphanages, children's homes, and schools, invalids, old people, and hospitalized persons.[12] Various industrial enterprises, administrations, scientific institutes, and other important organizations will also be ordered to leave.[13]

It has been recommended that people be instructed in evacuation procedures in peacetime, and especially that they be acquainted with the assembly points from which they would be transported in time of war. Those ordered to leave the city are expected to report at announced assembly points within 2 to 3 hours or less.[14]

Transportation will be carried out by all available vehicles, railroads, and boats. Motor vehicles will travel in convoys, and for every convoy or other means of transport there will be one person in charge. Usually, the evacuees will first be moved to "intermediate" evacuation centers situated 10–50 miles outside the cities; only later, and if time permits, will they be sent to their final destination in rural areas and small towns.[15] Presumably, this system is intended to speed up the initial evacuation and to move as many people as possible quickly beyond the blast and fire range of a thermonuclear explosion. Also, the authorities may not want people to be too far away in case the danger passes over and it is safe to return home. We do not know whether the "intermediate" or staging centers are designated in advance, or what shelter facilities against fallout they will have. The current training program instructs everyone to bring along some clothing, bedding, a first-aid kit, flashlight or candles, matches, soap, eating utensils, a pocketknife, individual means of protection, and sufficient food for several days.[16] More food will be issued at the intermediate evacuation center. At present, persons who have permission to leave may, if they wish, go to any district in the country independently of the organized transportation effort. If they do, they must first notify the evacuation commissions of their intention, and must provide their own means of transportation.[17] Except for people planning to walk to nearby villages, permission probably will be granted primarily to those with cars of their own. As the number of car owners in the Soviet Union is small, the independent exodus will not be significant enough to impede the organized evacuation traffic.

According to the manuals, any evacuation will be limited in scope, and a "large part of the population will remain in the cities and inhabited centers."[18] Nevertheless, it will require considerable time to execute. It is, in effect, to be a strategic evacuation, that is to say, one well in advance of a possible attack. The authorities recognize that an attack could occur while evacuation was in progress, in which event, people would have to take cover in shelters, just as they would in a surprise attack that precluded any attempt at evacuation. People already at evacuation assembly points would be directed to nearby shelters by civil defense personnel.[19]

In the event of an attack on the Soviet Union, an evacuation might be ordered under two circumstances: (1) in a likely target area, where it would have to be accomplished between the sounding of the alert and the detonation of a nuclear weapon, or (2) after an attack, when places at some distance from the explosion would have to be cleared before the fallout reached them. Concerning the first situation, a Soviet source mentions the possibility of a 1- to 3-hour warning period, which would permit the evacuation of cities if people were well trained and disciplined, if the roads were good, and if enough means of transportation were available.[20] Training exercises, says the article, are essential to ensure that people behave correctly and the procedures are smooth and effective. However, apart from the obvious difficulties of carrying out such an evacuation in any large city, Soviet transportation and road facilities for the most part do not meet the necessary standards. Furthermore, in these days of intercontinental ballistic missiles, the warning time may be so short as to rule out such an evacuation altogether.

The second possibility, of evacuating people after an attack and before the arrival of radioactive fallout, is only hinted at in Soviet civil defense literature. It is said, for example, that evacuation may be interrupted by an air-raid warning, but when the "all-clear" is sounded (presupposing that the particular city has suffered no direct attack), it is to be "continued in accordance with the established system."[21] Elsewhere it is thought likely that the "local civil defense organization will know in advance, on the basis of meteorological information, the direction of movement of the radioactive cloud"[22] and thus will be able to warn those threatened by it to take cover or to leave the area. Still another article suggests the possible evacuation of people and cattle from areas that might be affected by fallout.[23] The civil defense manuals themselves, however, place little emphasis on this type of evacuation, a possible indication that the authorities view its feasibility with less confidence than they do a pre-attack evacuation.

The need to remove people from highly contaminated areas is a basic concept of Soviet civil defense doctrine, dictated, as we have seen, because basement and emergency shelters will not be suitable for prolonged occupancy. Consequently, the civil defense authorities have been explicit about their plan to move survivors in highly contaminated areas to safer regions.[24] First to be evacuated will be those who at the time of attack are out in the open or in inadequate shelters, or whose shelters are damaged or threatened by flooding or fire.[25] The technical aspects of such evacuation will be discussed elsewhere in this book, but it is well to note here that the population is being trained how to behave in contaminated areas and in which procedures to follow in crossing them.[26]

Although the Soviet press has no reports of any citywide evacuation exercises, the experience of World War II is enough to indicate that the populace would require little advance notice of an evacuation. The orders might be issued by public announcement or in the form of written instructions from the evacuation committees to apartment-house managers and to the chiefs of industrial, governmental, public, and other institutions. Such orders would indicate only the category or type of persons subject to evacuation, the assembly point, and the time by which to report. The managers, in turn, would ensure that the directives were carried out promptly and correctly. They would be both supervised and assisted by Party organs, the police, and appropriate civil defense units. During World War II, entire organizations were evacuated in this manner with just one or two hours' notice.[27]

It is difficult to estimate the speed with which the Soviet authorities could execute a major evacuation of a large city. Since many Soviet cities are quite compact, and even their newer districts are built directly on the periphery, it might be possible for substantial numbers of residents to walk beyond the blast and fire zone. Evacuation would be further facilitated by the fairly well-developed urban transportation systems, by which people from the center of town could reach the suburbs rapidly and in large numbers. For travel beyond the city, railroads are still the chief means of transportation in the USSR, although the number of motor vehicles is increasing. Cities such as Moscow, Leningrad, and Kiev serve as terminals for a number of rail lines, and each thus has several major railway stations. (Moscow has nine, and Leningrad, five.) Furthermore, the largest cities have extensive networks of electrified suburban railroads, capable of carrying a great many evacuees.

In the event of an evacuation, the authorities plan also to mobilize many of the available motor vehicles not required for military purposes. In 1956 the Soviet Union had an estimated total of 700,000 passenger cars, 2,800,000 trucks, and 65,000 buses.[28] The industrial plan for 1957 called for the production of 113,000 cars, 371,000 trucks, and 10,300 buses. In 1960 this figure was increased to 130,000 cars and 385,000 trucks, and the current Seven Year Plan envisages a 440 per cent increase in buses by 1965.[29] It is not known whether the armed forces are to contribute some of their vehicles to the evacuation effort.

Not all vehicles would be available for evacuating civilians, of course; many of them would be in the rural areas, and others might be needed to deploy civil defense personnel within the cities. The efficiency of evacuation by motor vehicles could be limited by the extremely poor condition of most Soviet roads. (As late as 1959, the Soviet Union had only 156,700 miles of surfaced roads.) The areas around the largest cities, however, have some good highways that could be used to move people at least to the intermediate evacuation points. And efforts are underway to improve and expand the highway network.

The speed and success of an evacuation is likely to be affected by the seasons. Winter weather would certainly interfere with people's ability to move very far on foot. During World War II the Soviet authorities nevertheless managed to evacuate masses of civilians fairly rapidly, in spite of limited means and bad weather. Thus, during the siege of Leningrad, in the middle of the winter of 1941–42, an average of 10,600 persons a day were evacuated by truck over the ice of Lake Ladoga, despite German artillery and air attack, a shortage of trucks, and extremely bad weather.[80] In Moscow, when the Germans were approaching the city in October, 1941, nearly half a million people left the city within a few days, most of them by a single rail line.[81]

According to the civil defense manuals, present plans call for only partial evacuation of major cities, and some productive elements of the population will have to remain behind. The reason for this decision is not stated. Possibly, the authorities are anxious not to disrupt production and the economy completely, especially in the event that the "threatening situation" alert turns out to have been premature and no attack occurs. Perhaps the enemy is expected to attack only a few cities, either by his own choice or because Soviet military countermeasures prevent a widespread assault. It is also possible that total evacuation is simply believed to be impractical. In the event of an attack, urban residents who have remained behind presumably would have at their disposal the stronger types of shelters. Faced by the threat of increasingly large thermonuclear weapons, the Soviet authorities may of course decide to institute far more extensive evacuations than are foreseen in the present manuals.

It is difficult to tell how confidently the civil defense authorities are counting on the warning time necessary for a successful evacuation. The present shelter program is to some extent a partial insurance against the possibility of insufficient warning or total surprise. Yet the continuing and growing interest in evacuation, and the detailed planning for it, would appear to be an indication that the Soviet leadership is confident, or at least hopeful, of being able to assess the danger of war correctly.

8

Civil Defense Operations

The operational doctrine of Soviet civil defense, dealing as it does with pre-attack, warning, and post-attack measures, reflects the organization and training discussed in the preceding chapters. It is not designed for the worst possible contingencies, such as a massive surprise attack on a large number of cities. Rather, its premise, like that of the shelter program, is a relatively optimistic assessment of the severity of a likely enemy attack, and it has certain obsolete features. The doctrine may be said to be tailored to a given civil defense capability and to a modest investment in civil defense. Although it is being adjusted to new requirements, these adjustments tend to lag behind weapons developments.

The Warning Signals

Each of the several civil defense warning signals means a series of specific measures and actions to be taken immediately by civil defense authorities and civilians. The signals differ according to the character and nature of the threat.

1. The "Threatening Situation" Alert

The "threatening situation" alert (*Ugrozhaemoe polzhenie*) is one of the operational conditions of the MPVO. [It] signifies that the territory of the USSR may be subjected to air attack by enemy air forces in the near future. It is instituted by a decision of the government of the USSR so that measures might be carried out in time which will ensure the protection of the population and the operations of units of the national economy under conditions of attack from the air.[1]

This alert will be announced over the radio and in the press when the Soviet leadership regards an international crisis as sufficiently serious to make an attack on the Soviet Union appear possible. It somewhat resembles the orders for a military pre-attack mobilization in that it signals a variety of preparatory and preventive measures. These include the mobilization of civil defense personnel, the construction and readying of shelters, the issuing of gas masks and other equipment to the populace, fire-prevention measures, evacuation, the storing of individual food and water supplies, vaccinations against various bacteriological agents, and, in rural areas, the dispersal of cattle and the protection of food, fodder, and water against contamination and fire.[2] Many of these measures will be carried out with the help of civilians mobilized for the purpose.

Considering how time-consuming some of these preparations would be, the "threatening situation" alert, to be effective, must be able to count on many hours of warning time. That it figures so prominently among the Soviet Union's formal civil defense signals may be taken as a sign of considerable confidence in the possibility of obtaining, under certain conditions, early warning of an enemy's decision to attack.

2. The "Air-Raid" Alert

The air-raid alert is sounded when there is imminent danger of an enemy attack. It may be nationwide or local, that is to say, it may be initiated either by Air Defense Command headquarters or by the local air-defense forces, and will be transmitted to the population by the civil defense Warning and Communication Service.[3]

The air-raid alert is signaled by sirens, over the radio, and by factory, ship, and train whistles. The radio and public loudspeaker network will announce it in the following manner: "Attention! This is the city MPVO staff speaking. Citizens, an air-raid alert is announced! Air-raid alert! Air-raid alert!"[4] As soon as the air-raid alert is sounded, all residents must seek shelter. The rule against remaining in apartments or streets is strictly enforced by the police, the Service for Maintaining Public Order and Safety, and the management at places of employment and residence.[5] Before going to the shelter, every person must turn off all electric lights and appliances, gas ranges, and ovens, put out all fires in stoves and furnaces, and take along his gas mask, protective clothing, first-aid kit, food, and some drinking water.[6]

3. The "Chemical" Alert

The chemical alert is sounded if the enemy is suspected of having used chemical or bacteriological weapons or if there is danger from radioactive fallout. It is announced over the radio in a manner similar to the air-raid alert and is also signaled by striking gongs or pieces of rail.[7] The radio will specify the location and size of areas already contaminated and of those threatened by advancing fallout or the movement of gas clouds, and will suggest possible evacuation routes. The explosion of a nuclear weapon is also considered to be a signal for a chemical alert.

4. The "All-Clear" Signal

The "all-clear" is sounded by sirens and announced over the radio. However, it will not be given in areas of a nuclear explosion or in those contaminated by radioactive, chemical, or bacteriological agents, where it would be dangerous for people to leave their shelters immediately after the attack. Instead, the shelter commanders will be informed by civil defense reconnaissance and decontamination personnel when it is safe for the shelter occupants to come out. Once the all-clear has been sounded, the population and the civil defense organization revert to the status of the "threatening situation" alert.[8]

Communications

There is no evidence that the Soviet Union has developed a special civil defense warning system or special radio stations such as CONELRAD. Apparently, there is as yet no automatic radiation alarm system. The Soviet civil defense warning system seems to rely on the civilian radio and communication network, which would probably be supplemented by the air defense, army, and police communication facilities. One possible reason for the reliance on the civilian radio, rather than on a CONELRAD system, is that the large majority of Soviet radio broadcasts are transmitted to public or private loudspeakers over a wire system, which means that radio transmitters would not have to shut down during an attack for fear of providing a beacon for enemy bombers. In 1958, for example, out of a total of 39.2 million radio and television sets, 27.1 million were wire receivers.[9] The current Seven Year Plan envisages a considerable expansion of the radio and telephone system, including the completion of a radio and telephone network throughout the countryside.[10]

Local civil defense staffs and special units will probably have their own radio transmitter-receiver sets and emergency telephones for directing the operations of civil defense units in disaster areas. Shelters are likely to have either wire receivers or regular radio receivers, and special shelters may have been designed for use as emergency communication centers. These centers, as well as the local civil defense staffs, will thus receive damage reports and information on the movement of radioactive clouds, and will presumably warn any rural areas and towns that are threatened by fallout.[11]

Pre-Attack Measures

The "threatening situation" alert is the signal for a great variety of measures designed to reduce urban and rural vulnerability to attack and to make civil defense as effective as possible.

The actual value of a particular step will depend on the character of the attack. For example, urban fire-prevention measures will be effective if a nuclear explosion has occurred at some distance from the city, or in those parts of the city that are in the zone of light damage. They will be to no avail if the city is destroyed by a large-yield nuclear weapon.

Certain pre-attack measures—the construction of emergency shelters, the distribution of gas masks, protective clothing, and individual decontamination packets, the procurement of food supplies, and evacuation—have already been discussed. Some of the other steps recommended or ordered in the event that war threatens are examined under the following three subheads.

1. Blackout

Soviet civil defense doctrine still calls for a strict blackout in all cities and inhabited centers whenever there is danger of an enemy attack. Although this measure is designed only against a manned-bomber attack, and the Soviet authorities seem to realize that modern target-seeking and aiming devices can be effective without illumination or direct visual observation of the target, the effort is apparently still considered worthwhile, especially as it is cheap and simple:

> Under conditions of a contemporary war, blackout has played an important role as one of the means of protecting cities, industrial plants, and [means of] transportation from enemy bombers. . . . The use of such instruments [which allow bombers to locate and attack blacked-

out targets] does not ensure so high a precision in the destruction of the target as can be achieved with a sight using direct observation of ground objects and identification points.[12]

Although the views expressed in this statement may be valid when it comes to precision bombardment of small targets by conventional weapons, they do not apply to wide-area targets that can be attacked with high-yield nuclear weapons. Nor will a blackout have any effect on the performance of ballistic missiles, although it may be combined with measures designed to interfere with missiles that use infrared target-seeking systems.[13]

Despite the limited usefulness of the blackout, however, civil defense continues to require that all windows be covered by blackout curtains or shutters, all industrial fires screened, all outdoor electric lights shut off, the lights of motor vehicles dimmed, and so on. Compliance with these rules is enforced by the Blackout Service and the Service for Maintaining Public Order and Safety.[14]

2. Fire-Prevention Measures

To reduce the fire hazard to buildings, the civil defense authorities require the removal of all inflammable waste and stored articles from attics, staircases, and rooms located in upper stories; attic floors must be covered with a layer of sand or cinders, and any exposed wooden parts are to be painted with fire-resistant mixtures.[15] It is recommended that such highly inflammable objects as curtains, carpets, and soft furniture be moved away from windows to reduce the danger of their catching fire from the heat radiated by a nuclear explosion.[16] Inflammable outdoor fixtures such as fences or sheds are to be removed entirely. In rural areas, food, fodder, livestock, and fuel supplies will be scattered and protected against fire. Firewatches will be posted not only in buildings and factories but also in the country, where they will be on the lookout for field and forest fires.[17] Fire-fighting equipment is distributed in all buildings, and supplies of water and sand are held in readiness. As already mentioned, residents about to leave for the shelters must first extinguish all fires and turn off the gas and electricity.

3. Protection against Contamination

The principal means of protecting large numbers of people against bacteriological agents and the spread of infectious diseases are mass innoculations, strict observance of the rules of personal hygiene and cleanliness of homes and shelters, measures to control rodents, mosquitoes, and other pests, and isolation of persons suffering from infectious diseases.[18] The Soviet health authorities have had some experience with emergency mass vaccination. In January, 1960, for example, when Moscow was threatened by a smallpox epidemic, some 10 million persons were reported to have been vaccinated in one week.[19]

In the cities, the authorities and the people coöperate in protecting food and water against possible contamination. The municipal authorities and food distribution services protect their stocks of food supplies by appropriate storage measures. The water system checks on the purity of the water and may add filters against bacteriological agents. The individual resident is advised to wrap storable food in several layers of thick paper and to keep it in tightly closed boxes, refrigerators, or closets. He is also to fill bathtubs and other containers with water and then cover these tightly with sheets of rubberized or plastic material.[20]

In rural areas, food and grain must either be stored in tightly-closed rat-proof buildings or covered with tarpaulins if left in the open. Wells will be protected by covering them, and then surrounding them with a layer of compacted clay to prevent the contaminants from seeping down to the water.[21]

Considerable thought is given to the protection of livestock, especially against bacterial contamination. Apart from the shelters and even gas masks that are recommended for livestock, the plans include vaccination, dispersal, the covering of water and fodder, and other sanitary safeguards. In rural areas as in cities, watches are posted to guard against the contamination of water or food by enemy agents.[22]

Most of these pre-attack measures, though time-consuming, are relatively simple and inexpensive. Although the Soviet civil defense authorities may well realize the probable uselessness of these measures in any major target area, they continue to advocate them, presumably in view of their likely effectiveness in other parts of the country, and especially in rural areas.

Post-Attack Measures

In the event of an enemy attack, the guiding principle of Soviet civil defense is that the rescue of the injured and unprotected must begin "immediately following the appearance of a disaster center,"[23] and further damage must be limited as far as possible:

> In order to deal with such disaster centers, it will be necessary to organize, and carry out immediately, rescue and other urgent tasks. In addition, it will be necessary to organize the protection of people in areas that have been exposed to radiological, chemical, or bacteriological contamination. The lives of many people will depend on the speedy execution of such work, which will require much labor.[24]

Immediately after an attack, therefore, the entire able-bodied population near the disaster areas is mobilized to assist the civil defense organization in dealing with the damage. In fact, people are told to begin rescue operations and the fighting of small fires without awaiting the arrival of civil defense units.[25] This is presumably to be done in the time before the fallout begins to descend.

Wherever possible, the survivors of an attack will practice self-help, rescue the wounded, and fight minor fires. Simultaneously, the local civil defense organization, assisted by other units as they arrive from nearby cities and rural areas, are to conduct reconnaissance of the disaster area to determine the nature and degree of the damage and the number of persons requiring immediate assistance, so that appropriate measures can be taken to deal with the situation.[26] Later operations include evacuating survivors from shelters in heavily contaminated areas, decontaminating the terrain, aiding people who have been exposed to bacteriological agents, and protecting persons and livestock who are either in the path of radiological fallout or who live in rural districts threatened by chemical and bacteriological contamination.

1. Rescue and Medical Assistance

According to Soviet civil defense doctrine, prompt medical assistance in disaster areas is essential because (1) without it, many persons will die from their injuries, (2) rescue may have to be suspended when the area becomes contaminated by fallout or endangered by fire, and (3) persons buried under debris or trapped in damaged shelters obviously must be helped quickly.[27]

Civil defense planners and medical authorities realize that the large number of casualties is likely to overtax the medical facilities and the reserves of professional medical help. Their principle, therefore, is to have relatively unskilled persons administer first aid to those suffering from burns, broken bones, bleeding wounds, electric shock, concussion, and other lesser injuries, and to subject the injured to repeated screening (*triage*) as they pass through the various medical facilities, thereby eliminating the hopeless cases and providing professional treatment for those whose need is most urgent.[28] In the early stages of medical assistance, those suffering from radiation sickness will receive no attention beyond the decontamination of their clothing and bodies, because of the complexity of the treatment and the need for special facilities.[29]

Unlike other civil defense services, which are local in character, the medical facilities of the Soviet Public Health Service are organized on a broad basis, partly because no single local organization would be able to deal with the large numbers of casualties expected, and partly because many of the injured might have to be sent to facilities outside the disaster area for treatment. After an attack, therefore, all mobile medical units capable of reaching the disaster area within a reasonable time must proceed there at once.[30]

The disaster area is to be divided into a number of sectors, each headed by a senior medical chief who will coördinate the operations of search and first-aid teams, as well as those of the mobile and stationary medical units. The forces of a city's Medical Service are to be divided: those in the disaster area proper will consist largely of stretcher-bearers and first-aid personnel, who will give first aid to the injured and evacuate them; the professional medical units, stationed outside the disaster area, will give more thorough treatment to the rescued casualties. These units and their facilities will be organized in depth, so that as the injured pass through additional screenings farther from the disaster area, the treatments and services available to them will become increasingly elaborate.[31]

Soviet medical literature indicates considerable interest in aerosol vaccination techniques and in methods of treating radiation sickness. Work is also being done on chemicals that may provide prophylactic protection against radiation sickness or at least weaken its effects.[32]

The current training of the population in first aid, the large membership of the Red Cross Society (23 million in 1958), and the existence of numerous first-aid and stretcher-bearer units add up to a substantial capability for providing prompt assistance in the event of an attack to a great many of those who may suffer relatively minor injuries and can survive for some time without complex medical treatment. In 1958 the Soviet Union had 3,087,000 public health workers, including some 380,000 doctors and 1,300,000 nurses, medical assistants, pharmacists, and midwives.[33] Just how effective the survivors among these trained specialists would be in the aftermath of an attack cannot be predicted. In theory, the Public Health Service and civil defense medical services in the individual localities are responsible for stocking the necessary supplies, but there is nothing in the literature to indicate whether this is being done and how large such stocks are or are intended to be.

2. Fire Fighting

The Soviet authorities are greatly concerned about the danger of a major conflagration. In a nuclear attack, fires could result either from the heat generated by the fireball or from blast damage to buildings, gas mains, heating units, electric wiring, and the like. A civil defense manual says: "Fires resulting from secondary causes may spread rapidly and take on enormous dimensions, especially if measures have not been taken in time to extinguish them or to localize them."[34] Despite such references to fires of "enormous dimensions," the manuals avoid using the term firestorm. In fact, a civil defense pamphlet that had used the term was criticized for: ". . . repeating the version about the occurrence of 'firestorms' as a result of numerous fires following an atomic explosion. This version does not correspond to reality. It was invented by the imperialists for the purpose of frightening and scaring the people, and it is not necessary to refer to it in our civil defense literature."[35] The fires which have been described in some of the manuals, however, have all the characteristics that are commonly associated with a firestorm.[36]

By Soviet operational concepts, small fires in the zone of light damage caused by a nuclear explosion will be fought by the self-defense groups, and by units of the Fire-Fighting Service if they become large. Fire-fighting units in the disaster areas will be reinforced by special units from rural areas and nearby factories, settlements, or towns. Civilians and self-defense groups must use such simple equipment as axes, chemical extinguishers, and fire hoses, but the larger fires will be fought with heavier mobile equipment. A considerable effort will be made to rescue people from burning buildings.[37] In the rural areas, close watch is to be kept for possible forest or field fires, and these will have to be fought by the farmers with whatever fire-fighting equipment is available to them.

Although even the best-equipped fire-fighting units probably could not cope with large fires in the center of the disaster area, they might prove quite effective in the peripheral zone. It is not clear how these operations would be affected by radioactive fallout; presumably, they would not be attempted in contaminated areas.

3. Decontamination

Soviet civil defense planners assume that in a future war radiological, chemical, and bacteriological agents, used separately or in combination, could contaminate large areas. Hence they foresee a variety of measures for the decontamination of people, livestock, food, water, and other necessary supplies, as well as of ground and building surfaces and their contents, in order to save lives and restore affected areas to habitability and productivity.

The attitude of the authorities on the hazards of radiation exposure is similar to that in the West. Cumulative doses of 600 roentgens received over a short period of time are known to be lethal, and cumulative doses of 400 roentgens are expected to result in the death of 50 per cent of the people exposed. It is believed that severe radiation sickness and some deaths will occur at levels of 200–250 roentgens or above, and light radiation sickness with eventual recovery at levels of 100–200 roentgens. Under war conditions, a cumulative dose of 50 roentgens in a single day, or a rate of 10 roentgens per day over a period of 5–10 days, is considered permissible and safe. Such cumulative doses of 50–100 roentgens, though admittedly undesirable, are thought tolerable in an emergency because they are not seriously disabling. Any area showing a dose-rate reading of 0.1 roentgens per hour or more is consideraed contaminated. Several manuals, however, place the lowest rate constituting contamination at as high as 0.5 roentgens per hour.[38]

Although radiation levels begin to decline fairly rapidly through natural decay, this process, depending on the intensity of the contamination, may require from a few hours to several months before a safe level is reached. Soviet civil defense, however, does not propose to leave matters to this natural process, since it is undesirable to leave injured persons in contaminated areas unattended, and people in basement and emergency shelters cannot remain in them for many weeks. Also, the Soviet authorities are intent on restoring production in the surviving industry and economy as fast as possible, in support of the war effort and of the country's general recovery from attack. It thus becomes essential to decontaminate all radioactive areas and equipment.[39] As is pointed out:

> ... great significance is attached in wartime to the question of the economy and the rational use of material and technical resources. Under such conditions it is not possible to dispense with re-using the contaminated technology, clothing, means of defense, and other equipment. That is why it is essential to carry out measures that would make it reasonably safe for people to be in the contaminated area and would allow the use of contaminated equipment, technology, and food.[40]

Operationally, there are a number of stages in this process, starting with the partial decontamination of rescue routes and the treatment of exposed persons, and leading eventually to complete decontamination of the affected area and its return to production.

After an attack, special civil defense units will reconnoiter the disaster area to assess the extent of the damage and deter-

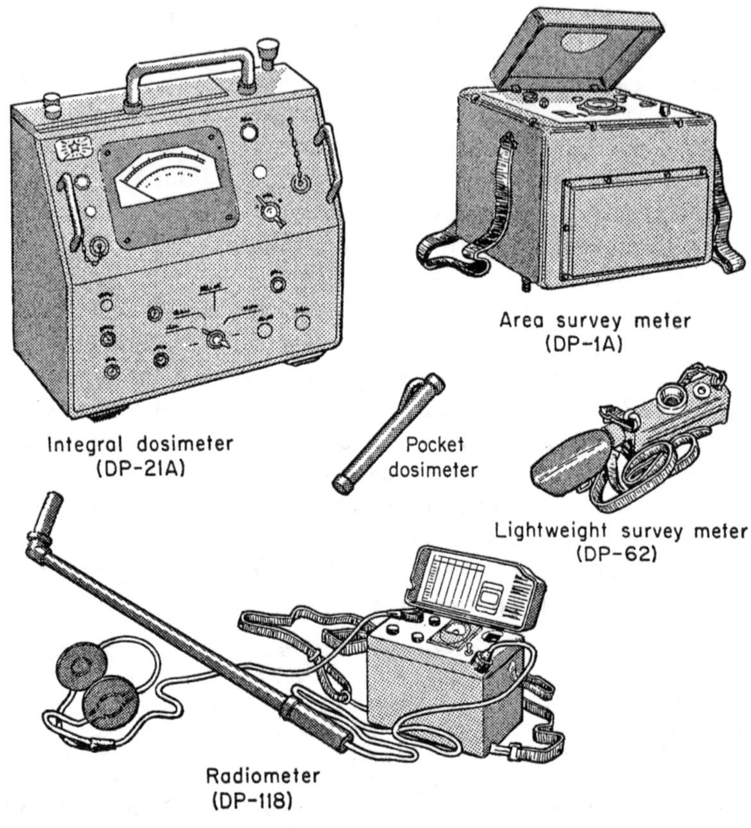

FIG. 22. Radiation detection equipment.

mine the most pressing problems. If they find indications of radiological, chemical, or bacteriological contamination, the local civil defense chiefs will organize special reconnaissance patrols to determine the extent of the affected area, the character of the chemical or bacteriological agent used, possible safe routes of approach, and so on. Each patrol will consist of two to five persons, equipped with the appropriate detection instruments, who will operate on foot, in vehicles, or by helicopters.[41]

Soviet civil defense has about a dozen different types of radiation detection and measuring instruments apparently of good quality and suitable for the task.[42] (For some of these, see fig. 22.) For chemical contamination, there are two types of chemical detection kits capable of testing for all basic agents including nerve gases such as tabun and sarin.[43] (See fig. 23.) Their effectiveness, however, is somewhat limited because they can test for only one agent at a time. A more efficient military detector kit may be made available for civilian use. For the detection of bacteriological agents, there are portable as well as mobile laboratories.

Even though civil defense training includes instruction in the use of radiation and chemical detection instruments, they are not to be distributed to the population in time of war. For the time being, at least, such instruments are to be issued only to civil defense personnel, including self-defense groups.[44] And, given the emphasis on public shelters and the continuous supervision over people's movements that is exercised by qualified civil defense personnel from the moment of an attack, a wider distribution of detection devices would in most instances not be necessary.

Once the extent and character of the contamination are established, the danger area is marked off by special warning flags and signs indicating the level and character of the contamination, and guard posts are established to prevent people from entering it.[45] Civil defense personnel who must operate within the area will wear protective clothing and gas masks, and will be under strict dosimetric control to ensure that they do not receive more than the permissible amount of radiation.

Residents evacuated or rescued from the contaminated area, and anyone else leaving it, will be checked for radiation and for exposure to chemical or bacteriological agents. The popula-

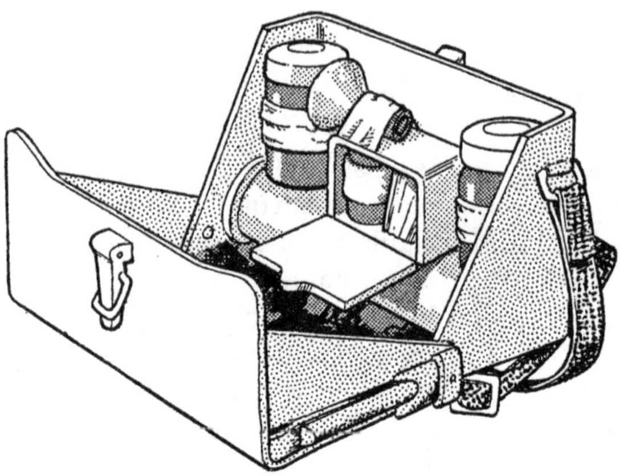

Reconnaissance kit

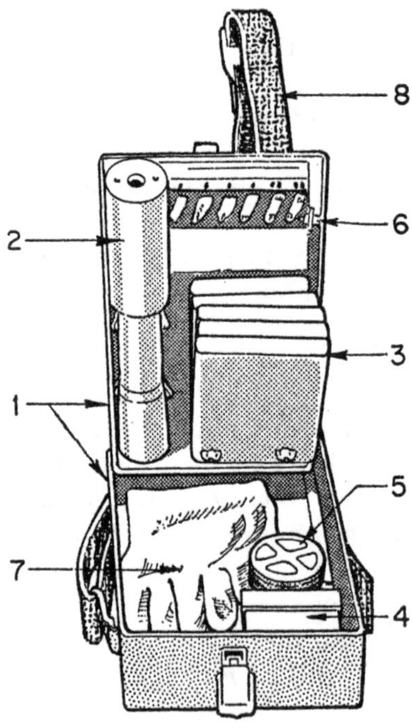

1. Hinged case
2. Hand pump
3. Indicator tubes
4. Smoke filters
5. Smoke filter adapter
6. Tube chipper
7. Rubber gloves
8. Shoulder strap

Simplified detector kit

FIG. 23. Chemical detector kits.

tion are already trained in safe methods of removing clothing, gas masks, and foot covering that might be contaminated, and they have learned how to use the individual decontamination packets. Those who are found to have been exposed will have to pass through decontamination facilities consisting of showers, laundries, and hot-air chambers, which will either be set up separately or attached to medical-aid stations. (Soviet sources indicate that much of this equipment is mobile and already available.) Anyone who has received an excessive dose of radiation, or who suffers from exposure to chemical or bacteriological agents, will be hospitalized.[46]

In the disaster area, partial decontamination is begun as soon as is practicable, and to the extent necessary to provide access and evacuation routes and safe casualty-collection centers. The operation will be carried out by the civil defense Decontamination Service, with the aid of military units and mobilized citizens. Wherever possible, the contaminated surfaces will be washed off, scraped off, or plowed under. Another method of decontaminating access and evacuation routes is to cover them first with a 2- to 4-inch layer of inert material such as earth, sand, cinders, or thick boards. (The passages themselves will be anywhere from 18 inches to 18 feet wide.) Later, heavy mechanized equipment—bulldozers, road scrapers, sprinkler trucks, or deep plows—may be used. Vehicles will be wiped with chemical solvents or washed with water and scrubbed with rotating brushes. The several decontamination kits for vehicles that have been developed (some of them quite elaborate) and possibly even distributed are yet another indication of the seriousness and thoroughness of Soviet civil defense preparations.[47]

Once cleared, the passages by which rescue, fire-fighting, and medical teams enter the disaster area will be used also to evacuate people from shelters if the area is unsafe for a protracted stay. In accordance with their training, the evacuees will don their protective clothing and gas masks, and civil defense workers will then guide them along marked routes to assembly areas, where they will be checked for contamination. From there, they will continue to safe, uncontaminated areas, where they must undergo complete decontamination by showers and laundries, and where they will be cared for by the civil defense Food and Trade Service. Thereafter, the evacuees either will be quartered in these safe areas, or will be moved back if the disaster area has meanwhile been decontaminated.[48]

Evacuating people from shelters before radiation has declined to a safe level, though probably unavoidable because of the limitations of many shelters for any but a relatively short stay, is not without risk in view of the hazards of passing through the contaminated zone. The passages are likely to be too narrow and their decontamination too superficial to provide a fully adequate shield against all radiation. Gas masks and protective clothing will offer no protection against gamma radiation, but will of course be useful against chemical and bacteriological agents. Much will depend on the level of radiation and the length of the passage through the contaminated area. Presumably, people in undamaged shelters will not be evacuated immediately after an attack, and the intensity of the radiation will have therefore declined considerably by the time evacuation becomes necessary, possibly three to seven days later.

The entire plan assumes the existence of uncontaminated zones relatively near the disaster areas. Whether such safe areas, which must serve as bases for civil defense operations and for the reception and quartering of evacuees, are actually within easy reach will depend on the character and magnitude of the attack. Overlapping fallout patterns from numerous nuclear explosions, for example, or the massive use of bacteriological weapons, could contaminate large areas and thus immobilize civil defense units and rule out any thought of a safe haven nearby. Therefore, if the Soviet concept of rescue and evacuation is to be workable, the attack will have to be relatively small and scattered so as to leave an appreciable amount of territory free from deadly fallout. It is impossible to say whether the Soviet authorities actually believe that this kind of attack is the more likely, or whether they have merely tailored their concept of rescue and evacuation to their present civil defense capability.

In zones of bacteriological contamination, a strict quarantine is to be imposed, and the civil defense training program is teaching people how to conduct themselves in such areas. Once the medical services have ascertained which specific agent has been used, they will coöperate with the Sanitation and Decontamination Services in treating the people in these zones.[49]

In the rural areas, the Veterinary Service is aided by the population in tending to injured or contaminated livestock, checking on the purity of food, fodder, and water, decontaminating buildings, equipment, and supplies, and evacuating the livestock from areas threatened by contamination. A number of relatively simple and cheap mixtures, equipment, vaccines, and special procedures have been developed for the decontamination of livestock.[50]

The civil defense Repair Services, along with other units, will concentrate during the initial rescue and evacuation on expediting the rescue of survivors and limiting the damage in the peripheral areas. In the next stage, with the Decontamination Services, they will proceed to the rehabilitation of the disaster area. Using anything from simple hand tools to heavy construction equipment, they will clear streets of rubble, help extinguish fires, repair water, gas, and sewage mains, and decontaminate streets, buildings, municipal and industrial facilities, and stocks of equipment. In the final stage, the citizens will be made responsible for decontaminating their personal possessions and the contents of buildings. This plan is consistent with the aim of Soviet civil defense to restore all remaining municipal, industrial, and transport facilities as soon after an attack as possible, and to rehabilitate the disaster areas for residential and productive use.[51]

Soviet civil defense literature has little or nothing to say about a number of important questions. We are not told, for example, precisely what measures have been taken to stock food and other supplies for an emergency, or how such supplies and essential equipment will be safeguarded. Nor is there any mention of a possible national recuperation plan that will reapportion the resources of undamaged areas for use in disaster areas. Nothing is said about what steps may be planned for moving supplies and men to critical areas, or how the leaders expect to preserve the political control systems. However, the lack of publicity does not mean that plans for these contingencies do not exist, for the literature tends to focus on local civil defense activities and recovery measures and thus permits little insight into over-all national plans. It is significant that in the past the Soviet government is known to have maintained large stocks of food, some in protected facilities, scattered in many parts of the country. Furthermore, the civil defense services, as was noted earlier, are responsible for stocking various supplies for emergency use.

9

Conclusions

The available evidence leaves no doubt that the Soviet leaders are serious about civil defense. For ten years or more, the Soviet Union has been engaged in an extensive and expanding civil defense program, which has already resulted in a significant capability. It is not a crash program, but one that seeks progressively to improve Soviet civil defense within the limits of a relatively modest annual expenditure of perhaps somewhere between 500 million and 1.5 billion dollars. Although the existence and direction of the civil defense effort are thus indisputable, we can only speculate on the reasons that have prompted this investment in civil defense and determined the specific character of the program.

Basic to an undertaking of this kind is the belief that major wars may occur in the future. This conviction was probably strongest in Moscow at the time when the Soviet Union did not possess nuclear weapons and had not yet recovered from the weakening effects of World War II. Since then, the Soviet leaders have been maintaining more and more emphatically that, with their growing power to deter the West from aggression, the probability of a total war has declined correspondingly; yet they are obviously not prepared to rely on this deterrent capability exclusively and under all circumstances. In their view, a danger of war remains as long as the East-West struggle continues, even though it may be progressively reduced as Soviet military power grows and the number of Communist countries increases. Moreover, they cannot be certain that the threat of war will continue to recede, for they are doubtless aware that the stability of any deterrent balance may be considerably affected by technological changes, and depends constantly on the military programs and postures of both sides, on alliance systems, the reliability and safety of retaliatory forces, and many other factors. Thus, despite the current thesis that total war is no longer inevitable, Soviet leaders regard the possibility that it may nevertheless occur as sufficiently great to justify preparing for it. Hence they have made a considerable investment in civil defense.

It would be a mistake to believe that the Soviet civil defense program is merely a carry-over from World War II, or that its character is the result of bureaucratic inertia unrelated to current military concepts or planning. In many respects, the program is markedly different from earlier ones, being geared to dealing with the threats posed by new weapons and strategies. New shelter designs, organizational forms, and operational concepts have been introduced and many earlier techniques have been rejected as obsolete. Nor did the present civil defense system grow directly out of the wartime program. It was launched a number of years after the war, and gained its greatest momentum after 1954, when the Soviet Union acquired its own nuclear weapons.

Even the fact that Soviet civil defense concepts apparently tend to lag behind the development of new weapons, thus rendering certain features of the system obsolete, is not necessarily an indication of bureaucratic inertia or of a military intelligence lag on the part of civil defense officials. The Soviet civil defense organization is not a truly independent agency, and any system it designs could hardly ignore the views of Soviet political and military leaders. Moreover, though its coordination with the Soviet military may not always be perfect, the close relationship between the civil defense administration and the military establishment is indicated by the large number of military personnel in high civil defense positions and by the support the program has publicly received from leading marshals of the Soviet Union. At the present time, the organization may in fact be completely under the control of the Ministry of Defense. It is quite unlikely, therefore, that the civil defense system would in any of its essential features go counter to the views held by the military leadership. Furthermore, under the Soviet system of central economic planning and resource allocation, the objectives and requirements of the civil defense program are subject to review by the Soviet leadership, who presumably would not approve the necessary investment unless they found the program desirable and in accord with their own beliefs. (The general agreement between military and civil defense thinking is borne out by the literature). Although Soviet military concepts are by no means rigid and some key questions are still being debated, the prevalent views of the military—especially on the subject of the protection of the armed forces—do not significantly diverge from those of the civil defense authorities. For example, civilian and military trainees are taught many similar defense techniques, including some that seem unrealistic or obsolete.

There is evidence to suggest that any backwardness in civil defense concepts and measures may be owing largely to considerations of costs and of priorities in resource allocation. Changes in the Soviet civil defense program tend to be anywhere from one to three years behind military reassessments of the threats posed by new weapon developments. Considering the time it takes to revise so large a program, as well as the obvious priority of military over civilian needs and the necessarily limited budget available for civil defense, such a lag is not surprising. It need not be construed as a sign that the civil defense authorities are unaware of new problems and threats or unwilling to take them into account. The very fact that the civil defense program, albeit slowly, has undergone and continues to undergo periodic revisions in line with changing requirements is evidence to the contrary. Although it is not inconceivable that a program such as this, once it has been established, may continue by a natural momentum despite changing reassessments of its worth or effectiveness, there is every evidence that the Soviet program has been steadily gaining in scope and complexity. More significant perhaps than periodic changes in the program itself are the indications of the government's increasing allocations of money and resources to civil defense. The leadership, which must balance such added investments against other competing needs, is unlikely to approve them merely to perpetuate an existing agency or its program. No such bureaucratic inertia has been evident in the other defense programs. For example, within a relatively short period Khrushchev has reduced the size of the army, eliminated large surface warships from the navy, and pushed the development of missiles and other new weapon systems.

Any suggestion that the Soviet civil defense program may be intended primarily as reassurance to a worried population, or as an adjunct of Soviet propaganda about alleged Western aggressive plans, is contradicted by the very complexity and costliness of the program. If its sole aim were to boost popular morale, it is unlikely that the Soviets would invest in a mass training program and expensive protective equipment and that they would inform the people in detail about the devastating effects of nuclear weapons or dwell on the dangers from chemical and bacteriological attack. The purpose would be adequately served by the relatively inexpensive construction of fallout shelters, without need for elaborate doors, filter ventilation units, and the like. In fact, the Soviet leadership could simply point to its growing military capability as a reliable deterrent and thus avoid large-scale civil defense expenditures altogether. On the contrary, however, the training program and Khrushchev's public statements on the destructiveness of modern weapons have actually run the danger of increasing people's apprehensions about a possible future war.

If the Soviet leadership is willing to make such a large effort, this must mean that its concern is not primarily with public morale, but that it regards civil defense as a significant contribution to the Soviet defense posture and as essential to the country's survival in the event of war. Indeed, the Soviet leaders have publicly acknowledged the possibility of a major war, in which they expect the enemy to attack industrial, administrative, communication, and transportation centers as well as military targets and to inflict great material damage and human losses on the Soviet Union. Their belief that in such a war neither side would have either moral or legal reservations about employing every kind of weapon is borne out by the substantial effort that the Soviet Union is making to protect the population, as well as its military forces, not only against nuclear weapons but also against chemical and bacteriological attack, and by the considerable civil defense capability against these dangers which it has already built up.

It goes without saying that despite the acknowledged destructiveness of contemporary weapons, the leadership is not prepared to write off the Soviet Union in the event of a war. Whether or not the Soviet state survives a major military conflict will depend on the character and magnitude of the attack as well as on the effectiveness of active and passive defense measures. Given the wide range of possible situations that may confront them in a war, and the technical and budgetary impossibility of creating a civil defense system that would be effective under all conceivable circumstances, the Soviet leaders have had to choose for which of these situations to design their civil defense system. Their military writers have mentioned the possibility of surprise attacks that would give the Soviet Union no more than a 15-minute warning, and they probably realize that a massive surprise nuclear attack on a large number of cities and economic centers could devastate the Soviet Union to such an extent as to make the survival of the regime highly uncertain and to preclude the nation's recovery for a long time to come. There is little that can be done in anticipation of such an attack short of providing full blast protection for the entire urban population, which would be extremely costly and difficult to do. But a massive surprise attack is not the only way in which a war may be launched. Soviet planners envisage other situations, wherein an attack would not necessarily be unexpected or overwhelming, and relatively cheap civil defense measures could effectively limit the damage and the number of casualties. Some military writers, for example, foresee the possibility of a war that develops more slowly and predictably and which may even become protracted. In such a situation the ultimate outcome could depend heavily on the speed with which the country recuperates from the main attack. It may be with a view to such a contingency that Soviet civil defense is giving priority to the protection of industry, administration, and Party. The same reasoning probably underlies the emphasis on measures that would limit industrial damage, facilitate the rapid recovery of disaster areas, and permit early resumption of some industrial production. To the extent that civil defense helps to contain damage and the loss of human lives, it improves the country's ability to survive a war and to recover from an attack. Hence, Soviet military leaders regard civil defense as a direct contribution to the Soviet defense and deterrent capabilities and as being an integral part of the country's defense posture.

Clearly, the authorities have been unwilling to make the

heavy investment of resources that would buy the best civil defense system possible. As already pointed out, they have not sought to provide reliable blast protection for the entire urban population. It is also evident that the present system will not perform very effectively in the event of sudden attack or even with short-term warning. Instead, the authorities apparently have chosen to tailor their civil defense system to a specific, limited range of situations in which a general war might begin.

Although a certain number of people could be effectively protected in a sudden attack, the civil defense system as a whole is clearly based on the assumption that Soviet leaders will receive considerable advance warning of danger. This is evident from the plan to build fallout shelters, evacuate the population, distribute gas masks, and take certain other protective steps only at the sounding of the "threatening situation" alert. But we should not therefore assume that Soviet civil defense is designed only against a manned-bomber attack, and not against a missile threat. These time-consuming measures could not be implemented at short notice to an extent that would provide adequate protection even against an attack by bombers. Soviet civil defense, as it is conceived at present, can reach its highest level of effectiveness only with many hours, or even days, of advance warning, even though every hour of warning time will, of course, add to its state of preparedness.

Soviet civil defense thus seems to be tailored, at least for the present, to the assumption that a war might well begin under relatively favorable circumstances. It is hard to imagine that the authorities would be willing to invest so heavily in the program unless they genuinely believed this assumption to be warranted. Although it might be argued that this may be largely a rationalization of the limitations imposed on the civil defense system by restricted investments, it is significant that this belief of the civil defense authorities appears to be shared by political and military leaders. On the one hand, these leaders (Khrushchev among them) recognize that modern weapons systems are technically well suited for surprise attack and that therein lies the greatest danger to the Soviet Union. Moreover, they realize that a total war could flare up suddenly, as a result of an accident or for other reasons, even though neither side had intended it to happen. On the other hand, while admitting the possibility of such situations, they apparently do not regard them as the only, or even as necessarily the likeliest eventuality, since the West is said to be increasingly deterred by Soviet military strength and retaliatory capability from attacking the USSR. Thus, Khrushchev declared in May, 1959: "The imperialists know our strength. To attack us is tantamount to suicide; one would have to be insane for this. I do not believe they are as stupid as all that; they understand the consequences that the unleashing of war against the socialist countries may have for them."[1] This view, Khrushchev maintained, was shared by the Central Committee and the entire government:

> Comrades, the Central Committee of our Party and the Soviet government believe that a situation has at present been created in which the imperialists will hardly dare to launch a war against our motherland, or against the countries of socialism. Our forces and those of our socialist allies are colossal, and in the West, apparently, this is now understood.[2]

According to a more recent Khrushchev statement, no surprise attack could "at one blow" destroy the entire retaliatory capability of a powerful enemy, who would "always have the means to give the aggressor a due rebuff."[3]

Although these threatening statements were clearly designed for their propaganda effect and are quite in line with the general attempt to deter the West from any military resistance to Soviet advances, it is evident from the Soviet Union's behavior and from its military literature that the leadership genuinely believes an unprovoked Western surprise attack to be at present the least likely of possibilities. Without denying that general war could break out suddenly with little or no warning, Soviet leaders apparently are more inclined to think that it would be preceded by a period of increasing international crises or by marked changes in the attitude of Western leaders and peoples toward the Soviet Union and toward war in general. An international crisis that deteriorated gradually to the point of general war, or a growing hostility and belligerency on the part of the West, could, they believe, provide the political indicators of Western intentions that would provide them with strategic warning of a possible planned attack; they would not have to await unexpected Western military moves, or preparations for immediate hostilities, for the short tactical warning that these would afford. Apparently, the likelihood of such a development is regarded as sufficiently great to warrant the considerable expenditures on a civil defense system that for maximum effectiveness depends on ample advance warning. The very existence of a formal strategic warning signal—the "threatening situation" alert—is indicative of the expectation that the events leading to a general war could provide such warning.

Past Soviet performance suggests that in some crisis situations the leadership has relied more heavily on political than on military indicators of enemy intentions. In 1941, for example, despite the German military build-up on the Soviet borders and repeated warnings from Western and other sources, Stalin refused to believe that Hitler would attack by surprise. He expected Hitler first to create a crisis situation that would justify an attack. More recently, in 1960, Khrushchev claimed to see in the U-2 flights, not an instance of Western pre-attack reconnaissance, but only an attempt to revive the cold war, whose intensity, he asserted, had declined as a result of Soviet efforts to relax international tension. Although Soviet leaders profess that Marxism-Leninism provides them with reliable "scientific" tools for the purpose, it would be difficult to say how confident they are in reality about their ability to make correct estimates of the chance that Western leaders might be provoked by Soviet actions during an international crisis into fighting a general war.

We must also consider the possibility that a steadily growing crisis might prompt Soviet leaders to initiate a preëmptive war against the West, or alternatively, that they may launch an unprovoked surprise attack without a prior crisis. In either event, they would thus have foreknowledge of the fact and timing of the war—the equivalent of strategic warning. The worsening crisis leading to a preëmptive attack would permit them to put into effect a number of civil defense measures without necessarily arousing the West's suspicions; a surprise attack, on the other hand, would probably rule out certain kinds of preparations, too difficult to conceal from the enemy, for fear that they might alert him to the plan and thus compromise its success. (The need for preparatory measures of this kind may, of course, be reduced in the future by improvements in the general state of preparedness of Soviet civil defense. It may then become possible to institute certain civil defense measures slowly and well in advance of the surprise attack in a manner that will not alert the intended victim.)

The expectation of being able to obtain strategic warning of any attack by the West may explain some of the operational concepts of Soviet civil defense. The large-scale rescue, evacuation, decontamination, and similar post-attack operations that are planned could obviously be successful only if the enemy attack were relatively small and scattered. For a powerful adversary to limit his attack in such a way would presuppose that his strategic forces had been severely crippled either by offensive means (that is, a preëmptive attack) or by an effective active defense, or possibly by a combination of both, and in these respects, too, ample advance warning of a possible attack on the Soviet Union would be essential. Again, it is entirely possible that further improvements in the Soviet shelter program will make the civil defense system less dependent on strategic warning and enable it to cope with larger attacks. The announced Soviet efforts to develop a reliable anti-aircraft and anti-missile defense could also greatly increase the effectiveness and worth of the civil defense program.[4]

The Soviet civil defense capability is potentially useful also as a political and deterrent factor. Although Soviet leaders so far have not injected civil defense into their threat and deterrence statements, they have cited the size of the Soviet Union and the alleged dispersal of its industry and population as factors that reduce the country's vulnerability to attack, and they may yet decide to exploit their civil defense capability for the same political purpose. (In this connection, an extract from a recent article on civil defense in a Hungarian newspaper is of interest: "In recent years civil defense instruction and practice were increased in the West. In the United States, civil defense practices are used systematically for cold war purposes and to create panic and hysteria. . . . Our preparations and the development of civil defense form an organic part of our effort at peace; preparing the homeland for defense means that if necessary we shall be able to protect our lives and materials from destruction more effectively. This in turn means that we safeguard and increase our forces and at the same time *raise hopelessness in the camp of the enemy. . . .*"[5] [Italics mine.]) Even if they do not openly point to their civil defense capability, the Soviet leaders may still derive certain political and diplomatic benefits from its existence: they may be more inclined than they would otherwise be to take certain risks in limited crises, and they may feel relatively safe in the assumption that their enemy will be somewhat constrained in his actions by the knowledge that the Soviet Union possesses such a capability.

It is not inconceivable that in a future international crisis the Soviet Union might institute various civil defense measures or call a "threatening situation" alert, in order either to underscore the extreme seriousness of the situation and thus strengthen the leadership's negotiatory position or to reinforce the Soviet deterrence posture in an effort to dissuade the enemy from resorting to military action. The obvious risk that such a maneuver could provoke the enemy into attacking may be one reason why the Soviet leaders have thus far refrained from it. Whether they make demonstrative use of civil defense in any future crisis will probably depend on their assessment of the likely enemy reaction to it. If they were convinced that the Soviet Union had achieved military preponderance over the West or that it had effectively impressed the West with its powerful retaliatory capability, the Soviet leaders might not be afraid of the possible provocative effect of a "threatening situation" alert, especially if the accompanying measures were introduced gradually and combined with appropriate political and diplomatic moves. They would be more likely to avoid instituting such an alert in circumstances where they were less confident about the probable Western reaction to it.

There would seem to be no technical obstacle to such a demonstration. The institution of a "threatening situation" alert would not in itself force any irrevocable decision on the Soviet leadership, and it could probably be maintained for a considerable time without causing an intolerable disruption of economic, social, or political conditions. For one reason, the authorities could control the pace at which various civil defense measures would go into effect, so as to reduce their disruptive effect. For another, present plans are already geared to the continuation of the country's economic activities under a "threatening situation" alert. Instead of calling for the complete evacuation of cities, for example, they provide for sufficient industrial, municipal, and administrative personnel to be left behind to ensure continuity of production. Moreover, a great many of the stipulated preparatory or prophylactic measures are simple and relatively cheap, and hence would probably not place too severe a burden on the economy. Also, since the evacuees are first to go to initial staging areas, and their movements will be closely controlled by the authorities, it would not be difficult or costly to return them to their homes when the alert is cancelled.

We do not know just how efficiently civil defense could perform at the present time even under the favorable conditions for which it seems to be designed. The system evidently has many shortcomings and certain obsolete features. Shelters are probably still insufficient to protect all urban residents and seem rare in rural areas, except for existing cellars. Some suffer from the limitations to prolonged occupancy, and certain types of shelters may no longer be considered effective. There is no indication that the present training program for the population has been completed, or that sufficient equipment and supplies have been stockpiled or distributed. Local civil defense officials have been accused of inefficiency, apathy, and mismanagement, and criticism published in the Soviet press reveals that the program tends to lag behind the official annual targets in some areas. At the same time, there are indications of continuous efforts to correct the shortcomings and adjust the program to new threats.

As of now, there is no evidence that the Soviet leadership has a set target date for completing the civil defense program and achieving a specific capability. Rather, the program seems to be regarded as a continuing effort to provide progressively better protection for the Soviet populace against an increasing number of contingencies. Such a system must of necessity be fluid and adaptable if it is to take into account new threats and problems created by the changing weapons technology. How successful it will be in eliminating its past shortcomings and meeting new needs is difficult to predict. It is evident and most significant, however, that despite the growing destructiveness of weapons and the necessarily limited effectiveness of any civil defense system, the Soviet leaders believe the program to be worth further efforts and continued investments.

APPENDIXES

APPENDIX **A**

*Outline of the 14-hour Civil Defense Training Course for the Soviet Population (1958-1960)**

FIRST NORM: *Present-Day Methods of Air Attack*
(1 class-hour)

(a) Means of attack, and foreign strategic weapon systems.

(b) Characteristics of atomic weapons and their destructive effects:

What is a blast wave, and what is its destructive effect?

What is the heat effect, and what are the defense methods against it?

What is initial radiation, and what is its effect on unprotected individuals?

What is radioactive contamination, and what are the methods of detecting it?

(c) How to determine the presence of chemical weapons and their toxic characteristics.

(d) Indications of the presence of bacteriological weapons and their toxic characteristics.

* *Uchebno-metodicheskoe posobie po provedeniiu trenirovok i priemu norm "Gotov k PVO" 1-i stupeni.* Moscow: DOSAAF, 1959.

Basic methods for the use of bacteriological weapons, evidence that a bacteriological attack has taken place, etc.

How infectious diseases are spread.

(e) Characteristics of radiation weapons.

SECOND NORM: *Individual Defense Means* (1 class-hour)

(a) Required knowledge:

Design and use of gas masks.

Improvised protective means and rules for their use.

(b) Required skills:

Using a gas mask correctly.

Determining the proper size of gas masks for oneself and for each member of one's family, and selecting (or adjusting) such masks.

Wearing the gas masks in "walking," "ready," and "action" positions.

Keeping the eyepieces of the mask from becoming fogged.

Protecting the gas mask and knowing how to use it under winter conditions.

Putting the mask on correctly from the "ready," to the "action" positions within 10 seconds (by persons up to 55 years of age) and 14 seconds (by older persons), respectively.

Wearing a gas mask continuously in a quiet state for at least 1 hour, or in a state of motion (at work) for not less than 30 minutes.

Using a damaged gas mask.

Putting a gas mask on a "wounded" person in less than 30 seconds.

(c) Improvised defense means and rules for their use:

Gauze and padded bandages (for covering the mouth).

Protective clothing.

Other means.

THIRD NORM: *Collective Defense Means* (2 class-hours)

(a) Required knowledge:

Proper use of shelters.

Responsibilities of the personnel assigned to service shelters.

(b) Required skills:

Taking refuge in a shelter in the required time.

Obeying and carrying out all established rules for behavior in shelters.

Making proper use of filtering and ventilation equipment in a shelter.

Laying out a trench or dugout under the instructor's supervision.

Providing an exit (both from within and from without) from a shelter buried under debris, using the simplest tools.

FOURTH NORM: *Fire Prevention and Fire-Fighting Methods* (1 class-hour)

(a) Required knowledge:

Aim and procedures of fire prevention methods.

The simplest fire-fighting tools, and rules for their use.

Method of summoning firemen when fire breaks out.

Methods of extinguishing incendiary agents and incendiary bombs.

(b) Required skills:

Carrying out fire prevention methods at home, at place of work, etc.

Extinguishing small fires, as well as incendiary bombs, by using water from hydrants, sand, barrels of water, hydraulic hose and bucket, and fire extinguisher.

Summoning firemen when fire breaks out.

FIFTH NORM: *Rules of Behavior for the Population in Response to Civil Defense Signals*
(2 class-hours)

(a) Required knowledge:

Rules of behavior upon announcement of the various alerts.

Measures to be taken after the "alert" is sounded.

Civil defense signals and their meaning.

Action to be taken upon issuance of the various civil defense signals.

(b) Required skills:

Preparing blackout equipment and blacking out buildings.

Carrying out defense measures in one's own apartment.

Carrying out sanitation measures.

Acting quickly and correctly upon the signals "air-raid alert" and "chemical alert" at work, in the street, in a public place, etc.

Protecting food supplies, water, and fodder against contamination by radioactive, toxic, and bacteriological agents.

Finding safe cover from an atomic explosion if one is caught outside a shelter.

SIXTH NORM: *First Aid*
(3 class-hours)

(a) Required skills:

Proper use of individual antichemical and bandage kits for first aid to wounded (oneself and others).

Providing aid in case of shock, fainting, and concussion.

Carrying injured persons in one's arms, on litters, and by improvised means.

Giving first aid (to others and oneself) in zones that have undergone atomic, chemical, and bacteriological attack.

Using various means to stop bleeding.

Applying tourniquets in case of arterial bleeding.

Applying splints in case of bone fractures.

Applying bandages to wounds or burns.

(b) Required knowledge:

Characteristics of injuries to people from atomic, chemical, or bacteriological weapons.

Methods of providing first aid to the wounded (oneself or others) in areas of atomic, chemical, or bacteriological attack.

Rules for the use of individual antichemical and bandage kits as well as of improvised means.

Rules for behavior in quarantine while under observation.

Sanitation measures for various types of attack.

Various means of providing artificial respiration.

SEVENTH NORM: *Overcoming the Effects of an Air Attack* (2 class-hours)

(a) Required knowledge:

Methods and means for decontamination from radioactive substances, gas, and germ infection.

Rules of behavior in the disaster zone.

(b) Required skills:

Decontaminating one's own house and household goods.

Decontaminating food products, water, and fodder.

Passing through contaminated areas.

Removing persons from under debris.

Proper conduct in a disaster area.

Correct ways of leaving disaster area.

EIGHTH NORM: *Veterinary Aid* (taught only in rural areas) (2 class-hours)

(a) Required knowledge:

Preventive veterinary measures in farms and at home.

Methods and rules for veterinary aid.

(b) Required skills:

Organizing the protection of livestock and poultry from enemy attack.

Stopping bleeding in wounded animals.

Applying splints and bandages to wounded animals.

Providing aid in case of burns and bruises.

Organizing the evacuation of animals from burning buildings.

Giving aid to animals that have been exposed to radioactive, toxic, and bacteriological agents.

APPENDIX B

*Outline of the 18-hour Training Course for the Soviet Population (1960-1961)**

FIRST NORM: *Functions and Tasks of the Civil Defense Organization When There Is Danger of an Attack and in Combating the Effects of an Attack*
(2 hours)

(a) Functions of the MPVO when there is danger of an attack:

Organizations and functions of the MPVO

Principal means of protection against weapons of mass destruction.

Duties of the population in response to warning signals.

Evacuation of the population, its organization, and the duties of the citizens being evacuated.

Sheltering and dispersal of the population; use of simple shelters in rural areas.

(b) Tasks of the MPVO in overcoming the effects of an attack:

Functions and tasks of the MPVO after an attack.

---

* *Uchebno-metodicheskoe posobie po prakticheskoi podgotovke vzroslogo naseleniia k deistviiam po likvidatsii posledstvii napadeniia s vozdukha (Normy "Gotov k PVO" 2-oi stupeni).* Moscow: DOSAAF, 1960.

Character and scope of the most urgent work in the disaster areas.

Principal methods and means of protecting the population from fallout.

Assistance by urban and rural inhabitants, and their direct participation in post-attack work.

SECOND NORM: *Duties of the Population in Carrying Out Repair and Rescue*
(3 hours)

(a) Duties connected with repair and rescue operations:

Purpose of the repair and rescue work.

Types of repair and rescue work in which the population may have to participate.

Special work problems in dealing with collapsed buildings and repairing the damage.

Methods of providing air to buried shelters, removing debris, and strengthening damaged parts of buildings and structures.

Methods of sealing off damaged portions of electric, gas, water, and sewage systems in buildings.

(b) Practical work in rescuing people:

Purpose and organization of rescue work.

Exercises:

(1) How to locate shelters buried under debris.

(2) Methods of rescuing casualties and extricating persons trapped under beams, debris, etc.

(3) Methods for removing casualties from buried shelters by the emergency exit (by hand-carrying, back-carrying, crawling, etc.).

(4) Methods of rescuing people from upper stories of buildings with the aid of ladders and ropes.

(5) Methods of evacuating people over partly destroyed staircases.
(6) Critique of the exercises.

THIRD NORM: *Duties of the People in Fighting Fires Under Difficult Conditions*

(2 hours)

(a) Purpose of fire-fighting.

(b) Characteristics of fires resulting from an atomic explosion or from incendiary bombs with napalm or "pyrogel."

(c) Methods of fighting fires with simple equipment.

Exercises:

(1) Putting out fires with sand.
(2) Putting out fires with water from a bucket pump or hose.
(3) Ways of removing napalm from horizontal and vertical surfaces.
(4) Fighting fires with chemical extinguishers.

(d) Methods of fighting fires outside and inside buildings.

(e) Practical work in rescuing people and removing property from burning buildings.

Exercises:

(1) Evacuating people from burning rooms by way of the staircase.
(2) Carrying casualties from a burning building through smoke.
(3) Rescuing people from upper floors of burning buildings with the aid of ladders and ropes.
(4) Removal of property from burning buildings.

(In rural areas):

(5) Rescuing livestock from burning buildings.
(6) Fighting fires in wheat storage or haystacks.

FOURTH NORM: *The People's Duties in Searching for Casualties, Giving Them First Aid, and Removing Them from a Disaster Area*
(4 hours)

I. First aid

(a) Purpose of medical assistance.

(b) Types of possible injuries in the disaster area.

(c) First aid for traumatic injuries.

Exercises:

(1) First aid for injuries to the temporal bone and back of the head.
(2) First aid to persons suffering from perforating wounds of the chest.
(3) First aid for a compound fracture of the clavicle.
(4) First aid for simple fractures of the 8th and 9th ribs.
(5) First aid for simple shoulder fractures.
(6) First aid for compound fracture of the humerus.
(7) First aid for hip wounds with venous bleeding.
(8) First aid for shin injuries with arterial bleeding.
(9) First aid for burns to the right side of the torso.
(10) First aid for dislocation of the ankle.
(11) First aid for fainting.
(12) First aid for heatstroke.

(d) First aid for burns.

(e) First aid for persons who have been exposed to chemical, radioactive, or bacteriological agents.

Exercises:

(1) First aid for hand injuries by liquid chemical agents such as mustard gas or lewisite.
(2) First aid to persons unconscious from exposure to carbon monoxide gas.
(3) First aid for head and hand injuries by radioactive agents.

(f) First aid for multiple injuries.

Exercises:

(1) First aid for head and leg injuries by liquid chemical agents of the mustard-gas type.

(2) First aid to a person with a shoulder injury, who has been exposed to hydrocyanic acid gas.

(3) First aid to a person who has been exposed to radioactive agents and has a simple fracture of the humerus.

II. Organization of the work of a stretcher-bearer team in a disaster area

(a) Functions of the stretcher-bearer team.

(b) Locating and removing casualties—organization and methods.

(c) Work of the stretcher-bearer team in the disaster area.

Exercises:

(1) Moving casualties by hand-carrying, shoulder-carrying, back-carrying, dragging on one side, and crawling.

(2) Having one or two stretcher-bearers move casualties by carrier-straps while crawling.

(3) Use of stretchers for carrying casualties with stomach wounds and with spinal injuries; how to carry casualties while climbing or descending.

(4) Improvised stretchers (using a piece of plywood, wooden board, or blanket).

(5) First aid for head wounds, and how to carry such casualties by hand.

(6) First aid for spinal wounds, and how to carry such casualties on improvised stretchers.

(7) First aid for an unconscious person, and how to carry him by means of carrier-straps.

(8) First aid for fractured ankles and hips, and carrying such casualties on stretchers.

(d) Carrying casualties from the disaster area by relays.

(e) Critique of this training phase.

FIFTH NORM: *Rules of Conduct and Action for the Population When Dealing with Radioactive, Chemical, and Bacteriological Contamination*
(4 hours)

I. External evidence of the use of nuclear, chemical, and bacteriological weapons, and rules of behavior in contaminated areas

(a) Purpose of training in this subject.

(b) Indicators of the use of nuclear, chemical, and bacteriological weapons.

(c) Ascertaining contamination by means of dosimeters and chemical reconnaissance kits.

Exercises:
(1) Testing soil for contamination.
(2) Testing well-water for contamination.
(3) Testing the surface of a building for contamination.
(4) Testing air for chemical contamination.

(d) The use of warning signs for a contaminated area, and ways of marking passages through and around it.

(e) Rules of behavior in radioactive areas and in those contaminated by chemical agents, as well as in areas subjected to radioactive fallout.

II. Rules of conduct for people in quarantine areas, and methods of caring for persons with contagious diseases.

(a) Purpose of the training.

(b) Rules of behavior in quarantine areas, and people's participation in combating bacteriological contamination.

(c) Helping to identify persons suffering from contagious diseases and those who are running a fever.

(d) Caring for a person suffering from an infectious disease in a quarantine area.

III. Decontamination work to be performed by the population

(a) Purpose of decontamination operations.

(b) Directives for carrying out decontamination and disinfection.

Exercises:

(1) Decontaminating chemically polluted areas by means of dry decontaminants.
(2) Preparing safe passages through contaminated areas for evacuation purposes.

(c) Critique of the exercises.

SIXTH NORM: *Examination*
(3 hours)

(a) Rules and methods of the examination.

(b) First Norm: Decontaminating an area contaminated by liquid chemical agents.

(c) Second Norm: Preparing safe passages through radioactive areas.

Exercises:

(1) Preparing passages with improvised materials (boards, beams, slabs, plywood, hay).
(2) Preparing passages by sweeping out the radioactive agents.
(3) Preparing passages by washing off radioactive agents with water.

(d) Third Norm: Rescue of wounded and other persons from the upper stories of damaged or burning buildings.

Exercises:

(1) Rescue of a wounded person trapped under a collapsed ceiling beam.

(2) Rescue of a wounded person from the second story of a damaged building by means of ladder and rope. (The casualty is conscious.)

(3) Rescue of a wounded person from the second story of damaged building by means of ladder and rope. (The casualty is unconscious.)

(4) Rescue of the wounded from the ground floor or basement of a building.

(5) Rescue of a wounded person from a partly destroyed shelter through the emergency exit.

(6) Evacuation of persons and casualties from a damaged building over partly destroyed staircases with the assistance of stepping stools and ladders.

(e) Fourth Norm: First aid to casualties and their evacuation from a contaminated area.

Exercises:

(1) Giving first aid to two casualties with a simple fracture of the clavicle and a twisted ankle, and removing them by means of carrier-straps.

(2) Giving first aid to two casualties with injuries to the temporal bone and chest, and removing them by hand.

(3) Giving first aid to a person with a spinal injury and moving him on stretchers in the presence of poison gas.

(4) Giving first aid to a person suffering from a simple fracture of the pelvis, and evacuating him on a sheet of plywood in the presence of poison gas.

(5) Giving first aid to two casualties (burns of the ankle and shoulder wounds with arterial bleeding), and moving them by means of carrier-straps in the presence of poison gas.

(6) Giving first aid to four casualties (injuries to the chin, wrist, shoulder, and knee) and evacuating them from contaminated area.

(7) Giving first aid to two casualties (broken ribs and chest wound) and evacuating them by means of carrier-straps from a contaminated area.

(8) Carrying casualties by relays and transmitting information concerning them.

NOTES

Abbreviations

DOSAAF	Dobrovolnoe obshchestvo sodeistviia armii, aviatsii i flotu (Volunteer Society for Assistance to the Army, Air Force, and Navy)
MPVO	Mestnaia Protivovozdushnaia Oborona (literally, "Local Anti-Air Defense")
MPVO v selskoi mestnosti	M. D. Korablev, Iu. Lebedeva, and L. Shesterikova. *MPVO v selskoi mestnosti* [MPVO in the Rural Area]. Moscow: DOSAAF, 1959.
Umpppv	*Uchebno-metodicheskoe posobie po prakticheskoi podgotovke vzroslogo naseleniia k deistviiam po likvidatsii posledstvii napadeniia s vozdukha.* Moscow: DOSAAF, 1960.
Umppt	*Uchebno-metodicheskoe posobie po provedeniiu trenirovok i priemu norm "Gotov k PVO" 1-i stupeni.* Moscow: DOSAAF, 1959.

[*Note:* For full references to works cited briefly throughout the notes, see Bibliography, pp. 195–200.]

CHAPTER 1

(Pp. 1–15)

[1] V. I. Lenin, "Report of the Central Committee at the 8th Party Congress," in his *Selected Works,* Vol. VIII. International Publishing House, New York, 1943, p. 33.

[2] N. S. Khrushchev, speech at the 20th Congress of the Communist Party of the Soviet Union, *Pravda,* February 15, 1956.

[3] *Ibid.*

[4] *Voennyi vestnik* (Military Herald), 1923, No. 17, p. 33, cited in Fifth Report by the Committee on Government Operations, "Civil Defense in Western Europe and the Soviet Union," House Report No. 300, U. S. Government Printing Office, Washington, D.C., 1959, p. 39.

[5] Fifth Report by the Committee on Government Operations, *op. cit.,* p. 39. See also A. S. Zubkin, *Individualnye sredstva protivokhimicheskoi zashchity* (Individual Means of Antichemical Defense), DOSAAF, Moscow, 1958, pp. 3–10, for information on the early development and manufacture of Russian antichemical protection equipment.

[6] *Za oboronu* (For Defense), 1946, No. 1, p. 24.

[7] Fifth Report by the Committee on Government Operations, *op. cit.,* pp. 96–97. Instructors passed a 50-hour course and were awarded the badge "Ready for Air and Chemical Defense, 2nd Grade."

[8] B. Stolpner, *Prevratim Leningrad v. nepristupnuiu krepost oborony* (Let Us Transform Leningrad into an Impregnable Fortress of Defense), Gazetno-zhurnalnoe i knizhnoe izdatelstvo Leningradskogo Soveta RKIKD, Leningrad, 1939, p. 26.

[9] K. E. Voroshilov, speech to the 18th Congress of the Communist Party of the Soviet Union, *Izvestiia,* March 15, 1939.

[10] A. V. Karasev, *Leningradtsy v gody blokady* (The Leningraders in the Days of the Blockade), Izdatelstvo Akademii Nauk SSSR, Moscow, 1959, pp. 58–59.

[11] *Ibid.,* p. 88. This official figure was far higher than the 63,000 civil defense workers who actually were available for duty in September, 1941, in Leningrad (Colonel M. Tregubov, writing in *Za oboronu,* 1946, No. 2, p. 11).

[12] A. Werth, *Moscow War Diary,* Knopf, New York, 1942, pp. 75–76.

[13] J. H. Meisel and E. S. Kozera, *Materials for the Study of the Soviet System,* George Wahr, Ann Arbor, Mich., 1950, pp. 366–267.

[14] *Za oboronu,* 1946, No. 13/14, p. 2. See also Fifth Report by the Committee on Government Operations, *op. cit.,* pp. 97–98.

[15] Fifth Report by the Committee on Government Operations, *op. cit.,* pp. 39–108; Karasev, *op. cit.,* pp. 87–88; *Za oboronu,* 1946, No. 23/24, p. 10

[16] Among the cities that were partly evacuated were Minsk, Leningrad, Moscow, Kiev, Sevastopol, Odessa, and Stalingrad. More than 1.5 million persons were evacuated from Leningrad (Karasev, *op. cit.,* p. 257), and about 1 million from Moscow (H. S. Dinerstein and Leon Gouré, *Two Studies in Soviet Controls,* Free Press, Glencoe, Ill., 1955, pp. 160, 182–186, 200–201).

[17] S. Volin and R. M. Slusser (eds.), *The Soviet Secret Police,* Praeger, New York, 1957, p. 160; *Za oboronu,* 1946, No. 11, p. 14.

[18] *Za oboronu,* 1946, No. 11, pp. 14–15, and No. 23/24, p. 10.

[19] Fifth Report by the Committee on Government Operations, *op. cit.,* pp. 63–64.

[20] *Ibid.,* p. 41.

[21] Fifth Report by the Committee on Government Operations, *op. cit.,* pp. 97–98; R. L. Garthoff, *Soviet Military Doctrine,* Free Press, Glencoe, Ill., 1953, p. 415.

[22] G. M. Popov and P. P. Reshetnikov, *Kratkie osnovy meditsinskoi sluzhby mestnoi protivovozdushnoi oborony dlia srednego meditsinskogo personala* (Brief Fundamentals of the Medical Service of Local Anti-Air Defense for Secondary Medical Personnel), Medgiz, Moscow, 1951, *passim;* I. I. Savitskii and P. M. Kirillov, *Protipovitriana oborona* (Anti-Air Defense), DTVU, Kiev, 1953, pp. 11–28; I. I. Savitskii, *MPVO zhilogo doma* (MPVO in a Residential Building), DOSAAF, Moscow, 1951, *passim.*

[23] *Voennye znaniia* (Military Knowledge), 1953, No. 11, p. 21.

[24] R. L. Garthoff, *Soviet Strategy in the Nuclear Age,* Praeger, New York, 1958, pp. 61–63, 156; H. S. Dinerstein, *War and the Soviet Union,* Praeger, New York, 1959, pp. 1–28.

[25] *Pamiatka naseleniiu po zashchite ot atomnogo oruzhiia* (Instructions to the Population on Defense Against Atomic Weapons), DOSAAF, Moscow, 1954, p. 32.

[26] *Sovetskii patriot* (The Soviet Patriot), February 13, 1958; V. D. Moskalev, V. P. Sinitsyn, and A. S. Tertychnyi (eds.), *Uchebnoe posobie po MPVO* (Manual on Local Anti-Air Defense), DOSAAF, Moscow, 1956, pp. 39–45.

[27] *Pravda,* January 15, 1960.

[28] Major General N. Talenskii, "The Soviet Disarmament Program and its Critics," *International Affairs,* 1959, No. 11, p. 8. See also Talenskii's article "On the Character of Modern Warfare," *International Affairs,* 1960, No. 10, p. 10.

[29] A. V. Bibergal and U. Ia. Margulis, *Atomnyi vzryv i nekotorye voprosy protivoatomnoi zashchity* (The Atomic Explosion and Some Problems of Anti-Atomic Defense), Medgiz, Moscow, 1958, p. 4.

[30] Colonel I. V. Kravtsov, "The Role of the Air Force in the Aggressive Plans of NATO," *Vestnik vozdushnogo flota* (Herald of the Air Fleet), 1957, No. 12, p. 80.

[31] *Pravda,* January 15, 1960. See also Khrushchev's interview with Henry Shapiro on November 14, 1957, as reported by TASS, *Pravda,* November 19, 1957.

[32] *Izvestiia,* May 10, 1959; G. M. Maksimov, "Movement and Composition of the Population of the USSR," *Istoriia SSSR* (History of the USSR), 1961, No. 1, pp. 31, 36.

[33] *Izvestiia,* May 10, 1959.

[34] Executive Office of the President, Bureau of the Budget, *Standard Metropolitan Statistical Areas,* U.S. Government Printing Office, Washington, D.C., 1961.

[35] *Izvestiia,* May 10, 1959.

[36] Marshal Zhukov, speech at the 20th Congress of the Communist Party of the Soviet Union, *Pravda,* February 20, 1956.

[37] Interview with William Randolph Hearst, Jr., November 22, 1957, *Pravda,* November 29, 1957.

[38] M. Dubinin and A. Imshenetsky, "The Danger of Biological and Chemical Weapons," *International Affairs,* 1959, No. 11, p. 47.

[39] Colonel I. S. Baz, "Soviet Military Science on the Character of Modern War," *Voennyi vestnik,* 1958, No. 6, p. 25; Dubinin and Imshenetsky, *op. cit.,* pp. 47–48; A. Imshenetsky, "Microbiology Must Not Serve Death," *Mezhdunarodnaia zhizn* [*International Affairs*], 1961, No. 2, pp. 78–79; *Voennye znaniia,* 1959, No. 1, p. 28.

[40] *Voennye znaniia,* 1959, No. 2, p. 28.

[41] Talenskii, *International Affairs,* 1960, No. 10, p. 26.

[42] Major General G. I. Pokrovskii, *Science and Technology in Contemporary War,* Praeger, New York, 1959, p. 50.

[43] Leon Gouré, *Soviet Civil Defense,* The Rand Corporation, P-1887, revised March 14, 1960. [Condensed version in *Air Force and Space Digest,* August, 1961, pp. 38–41.]

[44] Baz, *op. cit.,* pp. 24–25.

[45] P. Kapitsa, "The Task of the Entire Progressive Mankind," *Novoe vremiia* (New Times), 1956, No. 39, p. 10.

[46] *Pravda,* February 20, 1956.

[47] *Voennye znaniia,* 1956, No. 8, p. 12.

[48] *Ibid.,* 1957, No. 1, p. 4.

[49] *Sovetskii patriot,* February 13, 1958. See also Lieutenant General S. Shatilov's statement in *Voennye znaniia,* 1957, No. 1, p. 2.

[50] Pokrovskii, *Rol nauki i tekhniki v sovremennoi voine* (The Role of Science and Technology in Contemporary War), "Znanie," Moscow, 1957, p. 22.

[51] *Pravda,* October 25, 1961.

[52] I. P. Miroshnikov and G. N. Zapolskii (eds.), *Zashchita naseleniia ot sovremennykh sredstv porazheniia* (Protection of the Population Against Contemporary Means of Attack), DOSAAF, Moscow, 1959, p. 3.

CHAPTER 2

(Pp. 16–37)

[1] Miroshnikov and Zapolskii, *op. cit.*, pp. 81–82.

[2] *Ibid.*, p. 82.

[3] *Voennye znaniia,* 1958, No. 6, p. 18.

[4] *Pravda,* January 14, 1960.

[5] Marshal Voroshilov discussed civil defense at the 18th Congress (*Izvestiia,* March 15, 1939); and Marshal Zhukov at the 20th Congress (*Pravda,* February 20, 1956).

[6] *Sovetskii patriot,* February 11, 1958.

[7] *Krasnaia zvezda* (Red Star), January 10 and 18, 1961.

[8] *Za oboronu,* 1946, No. 12, p. 15; No. 23/24, p. 10.

[9] *Ibid.;* Fifth Report by the Committee on Government Operations, *op. cit.*, p. 47.

[10] Fifth Report by the Committee on Government Operations, *op. cit.*, pp. 46; 63–64; *Voennye znaniia,* 1958, No. 6, p. 18.

[11] Miroshnikov and Zapolskii, *op. cit.*, p. 82.

[12] M. Gvozdev and V. Iakovkin, *Atomnoe oruzhie i protivoatomnaia zashchita* (Atomic Weapons and Anti-Atomic Defense), 2d ed., DOSAAF, Moscow, 1958, pp. 157–158.

[13] Fifth Report by the Committee on Government Operations, *op. cit.*, p. 49; Major R. E. Aksim, CD, "Survival Operations in the USSR," *Canadian Army Journal,* 1960, No. 2, p. 17.

[14] Miroshnikov and Zapolskii, *op. cit.*, p. 81.

[15] Gvozdev and Iakovkin, *op. cit.*, p. 158.

[16] Miroshnikov and Zapolskii, *op. cit.*, p. 82.

[17] L. F. Supron and F. P. Zverev, *Meditsinskoe obespechenie naseleniia v usloviiakh primeneniia sredstv massovogo porazheniia* (Medical Protection of the Population Under Conditions of Use of Weapons of Mass Destruction), Gosizdat BSSR, Minsk, 1959, pp. 252–269.

[18] Miroshnikov and Zapolskii, *op. cit.*, p. 82.

[19] *Za oboronu,* 1946, No. 23/24, p. 10.

[20] M. D. Korablev, *Okhrana obshchestvennogo poriadka i bezopastnosti v usloviiakh PVO* (Maintenance of Public Order and Safety Under Conditions of Anti-Air Defense), DOSAAF, Moscow, 1960, *passim;* Miroshnikov and Zapolskii, *op. cit.*, p. 83.

[21] Supron and Zverev, *op. cit.*, p. 240.

[22] Miroshnikov and Zapolskii, *op. cit.*, pp. 83–84; *Voennye znaniia,* 1960, No. 7, pp. 33–34; Korablev, *op. cit.*, p. 7.

[23] Miroshnikov and Zapolskii, *op. cit.*, p. 84; *Voennye znaniia,* 1956, No. 6, p. 15.

[24] Miroshnikov and Zapolskii, *op. cit.*, p. 84.

[25] Volin and Slusser, *op. cit.*, pp. 157–158.

[26] Miroshnikov and Zapolskii, *op. cit.*, p. 84; V. D. Moskalev, V. P. Sinitsyn, and A. S. Tertychnyi (eds.), *Uchebnoe posobie po MPVO* (Manual on Local Anti-Air Defense), DOSAAF, Moscow, 1956, p. 48.

[27] Miroshnikov and Zapolskii, *op. cit.*, pp. 85–86, 120–122.

[28] *Ibid.*, p. 86; Moskalev *et al.*, *op. cit.*, p. 51.

[29] Miroshnikov and Zapolskii, *op. cit.*, p. 86.

[30] *Ibid.*, pp. 239–240; Gvozdev and Iakovkin, *op. cit.*, p. 160; *Voennye znaniia,* 1956, No. 6, p. 15; *Uchebno-metodicheskoe posobie po provedeniiu trenirovok i priemu norm "Gotov k PVO" 1-i stupeni* [hereafter cited as *Umppt*] (Training and Methodological Handbook for Training and Passing the Norm "Ready for Anti-Air Defense" 1st Grade), DOSAAF, Moscow, 1959, p. 80.

[31] *Voennye znaniia,* 1960, No. 10, p. 32; A. S. Zubkin, *Chto takoe dezaktivatsiia i degazatsiia* (What Are Decontamination and Disinfection), DOSAAF, Moscow, 1960, p. 21.

[32] Miroshnikov and Zapolskii, *op. cit.*, p. 85; M. Korablev, Iu. Lebedeva, and L. Shesterikova, *MPVO v selskoi mestnosti* [hereafter cited as *MPVO v selskoi mestnosti*] (MPVO in the Rural Area), DOSAAF, Moscow, 1959, p. 70.

[33] Gvozdev and Iakovkin, *op. cit.*, pp. 160–161.

[34] *Ibid.*; Miroshnikov and Zapolskii, *op. cit.*, pp. 87–88.

[35] Supron and Zverev, *op. cit.*, p. 255; Moskalev *et al.*, *op. cit.*, p. 53.

[36] M. E. Levin *et al.*, *Zashchita ot sredstv massovogo porazheniia* (Defense Against Means of Mass Destruction), Gosudarstvennoe uchebno-pedagogicheskoe izdatelstvo Ministerstva Prosveshcheniia RSFSR, Moscow, 1958, p. 110. See also Miroshnikov and Zapolskii, *op. cit.*, p. 88.

[37] Fifth Report by the Committee on Government Operations, *op. cit.*, p. 57.

[38] I. Gorbunov, K. Kotlunov, and V. Moskalev, *Deistviia grupp samozashchity i ikh podgotovka* (Activities of Self-Defense Groups and Their Training), DOSAAF, Moscow, 1957, p. 4; *MPVO v selskoi mestnosti,* p. 70; *Voennye znaniia,* 1957, No. 2, p. 22.

[39] Gorbunov *et al.*, *op. cit.*, p. 5; *MPVO v selskoi mestnosti,* p. 70; *Voennye znaniia,* 1956, No. 3, p. 18.

[40] Gvozdev and Iakovkin, *op. cit.*, p. 162; Miroshnikov and Zapolskii, *op. cit.*, p. 314.

[41] *Metodika podgotovki lichnogo sostava grupp samozashchity* (Method of Training the Personnel of Self-Defense Groups), DOSAAF, Moscow, 1959, *passim.*

[42] Supron and Zverev, *op. cit.*, p. 254; Miroshnikov and Zapolskii, *op. cit.*, p. 89.

[43] *MPVO v selskoi mestnosti,* p. 71.

[44] *Umppt,* p. 37.

[45] Miroshnikov and Zapolskii, *op. cit.*, p. 89.

[46] *MPVO v selskoi mestnosti,* p. 71.

[47] Miroshnikov and Zapolskii, *op. cit.*, pp. 237–238; Gvozdev and Iakovkin, *op. cit.*, p. 160.

[48] *Krasnaia zvezda,* September 26, 1957.

[49] See, for example, *Sovetskii patriot,* May 20, 1959; *Voennye znaniia,* 1958, No. 3, p. 32, and No. 11, p. 5; 1959, No. 8, p. 8.

[50] See, for example, *Sovetskii patriot,* August 11, November 24, 1957; June 11, 1958; May 17, September 6 and 16, 1959; *Voennye znaniia,* 1957, No. 12, p. 33; 1959, No. 2, p. 30, and No. 3, pp. 31–32; *Sovetskii krasnyi krest* (Soviet Red Cross), 1957, No. 5.

[51] *Sovetskii patriot,* April 9, 1958.

[52] See, for example, *Voennye znaniia,* 1957, No. 12, p. 33; 1959, No. 2, p. 30, and No. 3, pp. 31–32; *Sovetskii patriot,* August 11, November 24, 1957; June 11, 1958; May 17, September 6 and 16, 1959; August 16, 1961.

[53] H. Schellhammer, "Die Problematik des Luftschutzes im Atomzeitalter," *Wehrkunde,* 1959, No. 3, p. 145; see also Major Aksim, *op. cit.,* p. 18; The Honorable Clyde Doyle, *Appendix, Congressional Record,* February 20, 1961, pp. A-1078–1079.

[54] Major Aksim, *op. cit.,* p. 18.

[55] Gorbunov *et al., op. cit.,* p. 5; *Voennye znaniia,* 1956, No. 3, p. 18; Levin *et al., op. cit.,* p. 111.

[56] *Sovetskii patriot,* February 12–26, 1958.

[57] *Ibid.,* July 5 and 8, October 7, November 4 and 11, 1959; February 14, March 27, December 25 and 28, 1960; *Voennye znaniia,* 1957, No. 2, pp. 23–25, and No. 6, pp. 12–13.

[58] *Sovetskii patriot,* November 4, 1959.

[59] *Ibid.,* July 5, September 30, October 7, November 4, 1959; February 14, March 27, December 25 and 28, 1960; *Voennye znaniia,* 1957, No. 2, pp. 23–25, and No. 6, pp. 12–13.

[60] *Sovetskii patriot,* February 14, March 2, November 10, 1960; *Komsomol i DOSAAF* (The Komsomol and DOSAAF), Molodaiia Gvardiia, Moscow, 1954, *passim.*

[61] Fifth Report by the Committee on Government Operations, *op. cit.,* p. 46, n. 52.

[62] *Ibid.,* p. 58; *Sovetskii patriot,* April 9, 1958.

[63] Gvozdev and Iakovkin, *op. cit.,* p. 165; *Voennye znaniia,* 1958, No. 7, p. 26.

[64] Miroshnikov and Zapolskii, *op. cit.,* p. 160.

[65] *Sovetskii patriot,* March 8, 1959.

[66] *Ibid.,* April 29, 1959.

[67] *The New York Times,* May 17, 1961. See also Hearings Before the Subcommittee of the Committee on Appropriations, House of Representatives, Eighty-seventh Congress, First Session, *Independent Offices Appropriations for 1962,* U.S. Government Printing Office, Washington, D.C., 1961, p. 851.

CHAPTER 3

(Pp. 38–61)

[1] Bibergal and Margulis, *op. cit.*, pp. 4–5; *Sovetskii patriot*, August 9, 1959; *Voennye znaniia*, 1960, No. 10, p. 32; *Uchebno-metodicheskoe posobie po prakticheskoi podgotovke vzroslogo naseleniia k deistviiam po likvidatsii posledstvii napadeniia s vozdukha* [hereafter cited as *Umpppv*] (Training and Methodological Handbook for Conducting Practical Preparation of the Adult Population for Action in Liquidating the Consequences of an Attack from the Air), DOSAAF, Moscow, 1960, pp. 3–4.

[2] *Voennye znaniia*, 1956, No. 8, p. 12.

[3] *Ibid.*, 1957, No. 2, p. 3.

[4] *Sovetskii patriot*, February 13, 1958.

[5] *Voennye znaniia*, 1957, No. 1, pp. 2, 4.

[6] R. L. Garthoff, *Soviet Strategy in the Nuclear Age*, p. 45.

[7] *Voennye znaniia*, 1954, No. 5, p. 11.

[8] *Sovetskii patriot*, May 1, October 19, 1958; "Soviet Civil Defense Against CBR Attack," *Armed Forces Chemical Journal*, May–June, 1959, No. 3, p. 16.

[9] *Sovetskii patriot*, September 14, 1958; March 18, April 19, 1959; February 14, 1960; *Voennye znaniia*, 1959, No. 10, p. 2.

[10] *Voennye znaniia*, 1959, No. 10, p. 3.

[11] *Ibid.*, 1961, No. 1, p. 1, and No. 2, p. 4.

[12] *Krasnaia zvezda*, January 23, 1957; *Sovetskii patriot*, 1958–1961, *passim; Voennye znaniia*, 1956, No. 6, p. 19.

[13] *Sputnik komsomolskogo aktivista* (Companion of the Komsomol Activist), Molodaia Gvardiia, Moscow, 1960, p. 41.

[14] *Bolshaia sovetskaia entsiklopediia* (Great Soviet Encyclopedia), 2d ed., vol. 40, Gosudarstvennoe nauchnoe izdatelstvo "Bolshaia sovetskaia entsiklopediia," Moscow, 1957, p. 223; Gorbunov *et al.*, *op. cit.*, p. 72; Supron and Zverev, *op. cit.*, pp. 251–255.

[15] *Umpppv*, p. 5.

[16] *Sovetskii krasnyi krest*, 1957, No. 2.

[17] Fifth Report by the Committee on Government Operations, p. 103; *Sovetskii patriot*, January 10, 1960; *Voennye znaniia*, 1961, No. 3, p. 17.

[18] *Sovetskii patriot*, November 13, December 21 and 25, 1960; February 12, 1961; *Voennye znaniia*, 1960, No. 2, p. 35; K. Kipriian, *Kak organizovat priem norm "Gotov k PVO" vtoroi stupeni* (How to Organize Examinations of the Course "Ready for Anti-Air Defense," Second Grade), DOSAAF, Moscow, 1960, p. 55.

[19] See, for example, *Sovietskii patriot*, February 14, 1961.

[20] See, for example, *ibid.*, September 23, November 22 and 30, 1959; May 25, November 30, 1960; February 8, 1961.

[21] *Ibid.*, February 15, May 6, 10, and 13, July 8, December 2 and 16, 1959; March 16 and 30, 1960; August 20, 1961.

[22] Miroshnikov and Zapolskii, *op. cit.*, pp. 329–330; *Metodika podgotovki lichnogo sostava grupp samozashchity*, pp. 165–166; *Voennye znaniia*, 1957, No. 3, p. 39; *Sovetskii patriot*, October 1, 1961.

[23] *Umpppv, passim;* Kipriian, *op. cit.*, p. 26.

[24] See, for example, *Voennye znaniia*, 1957, No. 12 (enclosure); 1958, No. 6, pp. 16–17; 1960, No. 2, p. 35; *Sovetskii patriot*, October 19, 1958; September 2 and 27, 1959; February 17, April 3, May 25, October 2, 1960.

[25] See, for example, *ibid.*, March 8, 1959; January 20, February 28, March 20, October 2, 1960; January 29, February 19, 1961.

[26] Fifth Report by the Committee on Government Operations, p. 99; *Sovietskii patriot*, February 12, 1958; Moskalev *et al.*, *op. cit.*, p. 58; M. P. Arkhipov, *Osnovy ustroistva atomnogo oruzhiia i protivoatomnaia zashchita* (Basic Principles of Atomic Weapons and Anti-Atomic Defense), DOSAAF, Moscow, 1956, *passim;* P. M. Kirillov, *Dosaafovtsu o MPVO* (To the DOSAAF Member on Local Anti-Air Defense), DOSAAF, Moscow, 1956, *passim.*

[27] *Voennye znaniia*, 1955, No. 8, p. 26, and No. 12, pp. 18–19; 1956, No. 2, p. 26; No. 3, p. 18; No. 6, pp. 16–17; No. 7, pp. 11–12; No. 9, p. 26; and No. 10, p. 31; Moskalev *et al.*, *op. cit.*, *passim;* Kirillov, *op. cit.*, *passim.*

[28] *Sovetskii patriot*, February 12, 1958.

[29] Moskalev *et al.*, *op. cit.*, pp. 8–45; *Pamiatka naseleniiu po zashchite ot atomnogo, khimichsekogo i bakteriologicheskogo oruzhiia* (Instruction to the Population on Defense Against Atomic, Chemical, and Bacteriological Weapons), DOSAAF, Moscow, 1957, pp. 4–20; Iu. Lebedeva and V. Serebriakov, *Bakteriologicheskoe oruzhie inostrannykh armii i zashchita ot nego* (Bacteriological Weapons of Foreign Armies and Defense Against Them), DOSAAF, Moscow, 1957, *passim;* A. Malshinskii, *Khimicheskoe oruzhie inostrannykh armii i protivokhimicheskaia zashchita* (Chemical Weapons of Foreign Armies and Anti-Chemical Defense), DOSAAF, Moscow, 1957, *passim.*

[30] *Ibid.;* I. P. Miroshnikov, *Kollektivnye sredstva protivoatomnoi zashchity* (Collective Means of Anti-Atomic Defense), DOSAAF, Moscow, 1951, *passim; Voennye znaniia*, 1957, No. 1, pp. 24–25.

[31] *Sovetskii patriot*, May 20, 1959.

[32] *Ibid.*, 1957–1959, *passim.*

[33] *Ibid.*, May 20, October 22, November 30, 1959.

[34] *Voennye znaniia*, 1958, No. 10, p. 32; *Sovetskii patriot*, February 26, 1958; *Umppt, passim.*

[35] *Voennye znaniia*, 1958, No. 3, p. 32.

[36] *Umppt, passim.*

[37] Miroshnikov and Zapolskii, *op. cit.*, pp. 6–8; Levin *et al.*, *op. cit.*, pp. 5–9.

[38] Miroshnikov and Zapolskii, *op. cit.*, pp. 8–9; Supron and Zverev, *op. cit.*, p. 16.

[39] Levin *et al.*, *op. cit.*, pp. 30–35; Iu. A. Lebedeva (ed.), *Sredstva i sposoby protivovozdushnoi oborony naseleniia* (Means and Methods for Anti-Air Defense of the Population), DOSAAF, Moscow, 1958, p. 6; Supron and

Zverev, *op. cit.*, pp. 86–88; Gvozdev and Iakovkin, *op. cit.*, p. 142; A. V. Koslova, *Posledstviia vzryvov atomnykh bomb v Khirosima i Nagasaki i vodorodnoi bomby v Bikini* (The Consequences of Explosions of Atomic Bombs in Hiroshima and Nagasaki and of a Hydrogen Bomb in Bikini), Medgiz, Moscow, 1957, *passim.*

[40] *Umppt,* p. 13. See also Levin *et al.*, *op. cit.*, p. 39; Miroshnikov and Zapolskii, *op. cit.*, p. 43; Kirillov, *op. cit.*, p. 29; Moskalev *et al.*, *op. cit.*, p. 38; G. F. Baratov, *Mestnaia protivovozdushnaia oborna naseleniia v usloviiakh khimicheskogo, atomnogo i bakteriologicheskogo napadeniia* (Local Anti-Air Defense of the Population Under Conditions of Chemical, Atomic and Bacteriological Attack), Gosizdat meditsinskoe izdatelstvo USSR, Kiev, 1959, p. 72; *Sovetskii patriot,* June 10, 1959.

[41] M. V. Neiman and K. M. Sadilenko, *Termoiadernoe oruzhie* (Thermonuclear Weapons), Voenizdat Ministerstva Oborony Soiuza SSR, Moscow, 1958, pp. 138–139.

[42] Gvozdev and Iakovkin, *op. cit.*, pp. 38, 109.

[43] *MPVO v selskoi mestnosti,* p. 23; Supron and Zverev, *op. cit.*, p. 93.

[44] See, for example, Lebedeva, *op. cit.*, p. 10; T. V. Dolbnin, *Bakteriologicheskoe oruzhie i mery zashchity ot nego* (Bacteriological Weapons and Defense Measures Against Them), DOSAAF, Moscow, 1959, p. 5.

[45] Miroshnikov and Zapolskii, *op. cit.*, pp. 47–55, 63–77, 310–313; Levin *et al.*, *op. cit.*, pp. 53–59.

[46] *Umppt,* p. 14.

[47] *Ibid.*, p. 74; *Metodika podgotovki lichnogo sostava grupp samozashchity,* p. 46.

[48] *Voennye znaniia,* 1958, No. 3, p. 32; 1959, No. 1, pp. 29–31, and No. 8, p. 8; *Armed Forces Chemical Journal,* pp. 16–18.

[49] Miroshnikov and Zapolskii, *op. cit.*, pp. 44–47; Levin *et al.*, *op. cit.*, pp. 39–40; *Umppt,* p. 13.

[50] *Sovetskii patriot,* 1959–1960, *passim.*

[51] *Ibid.*, February 12, 1961.

[52] *Kipriian, op. cit.*, pp. 3, 4. See also *Voennye znaniia,* 1959, No. 12, p. 9; *Umpppv, passim.*

[53] *Umpppv,* pp. 4, 13, 35; *Voennye znaniia,* 1959, No. 12, p. 9.

[54] *Umpppv,* p. 33.

[55] *Voennye znaniia,* 1961, No. 1, p. 39.

[56] *Umpppv,* p. 24. See also *Voennye znaniia,* 1960, No. 7, pp. 33–34.

[57] Miroshnikov and Zapolskii, *op. cit.*, p. 82; Gvozdev and Iakovkin, *op. cit.*, p. 159.

[58] *Umpppv,* p. 9; *Voennye znaniia,* 1961, No. 1, pp. 31–32; *Sovetskii patriot,* February 12, 1961.

[59] *Umpppv,* pp. 27, 51.

[60] B. Stavrov, *Rabota voditelia avtomobilia v usloviiakh primeneniia atomnogo, khimicheskogo i bakteriologicheskogo oruzhiia* (The Work of Drivers of Automobiles Under Conditions of Atomic, Chemical, and Bacteriological Weapons Employment), DOSAAF, Moscow, 1960, *passim; Sovetskii patriot,* December 16, 1959.

[61] *Voennye znaniia,* 1961, No. 1, p. 1.

[62] *Umpppv,* p. 5; N. Ivanov, *Bud gotov k PVO* (Be Ready for Anti-Air Defense), DOSAAF, Moscow, 1959, pp. 4–5.

[63] *Sovetskii patriot,* December 25, 1960; January 21, February 5, 12, and 19, October 1, 1961.

[64] *Voennye znaniia,* 1961, No. 1, p. 31. See also *Sovetskii patriot,* February 12, 1961.

[65] See, for example, *Voennye znaniia,* 1958, No. 12, pp. 20–21; 1959, No. 3, pp. 31–32, and No. 4, pp. 34–35; *Sovetskii patriot,* August 11, 1957; June 11, August 6, 1958; May 20, 1959.

[66] *Voennye znaniia,* 1958, No. 7, p. 26; Miroshnikov and Zapolskii, *op. cit.,* pp. 331–333; *Sovetskii patriot,* September 2 and 13, October 22, 1959; February 14, November 10, 1960.

[67] Meisel and Kozera, *op. cit.,* pp. 366–367.

[68] *Leningradskaia pravda,* July 29, 1941.

[69] *Sovetskii patriot,* December 23, 1959. See also April 6, 1960.

[70] *Ibid.,* December 23, 1959.

[71] *Magyar Kozloni* (Hungarian Message), No. 112, December 18, 1960.

[72] *Voennye znaniia,* 1958, No. 6, p. 1.

[73] *Sovetskii patriot,* July 8, 1959.

[74] *Ibid.,* December 2, 1959.

[75] *Ibid.,* July 29, 1959. See also August 9, 1959, and March 13, 1960.

[76] *Ibid.,* April 6, 1960.

[77] *Ibid.,* March 13, 1960.

[78] *Ibid.,* April 27, 1960.

CHAPTER 4

(Pp. 62–70)

[1] *Sovetskaia aviatsiia* (Soviet Aviation), August 12, 1958.

[2] *Pravda,* October 25, 1959. See also *Soviet News,* June 9, 1960.

[3] *Izvestiia,* August 7, 1958.

[4] Alexei Kudriavtsev, "Care of Man Is the Basis of Soviet City Planning," Press Department release No. 353, Embassy of the USSR, Washington, D.C., July 21, 1960.

[5] *Ibid.; Pravda,* May 10, 1959.

[6] D. Khodjaiev, "Villes de Demain," *Études Sovietiques,* March 1961, No. 156, p. 42.

[7] Miroshnikov and Zapolskii, *op. cit.,* p. 92.

[8] *Pravda,* February 15, 1956.

[9] *Ibid.,* October 25, 1959.

[10] Gvozdev and Iakovkin, *op. cit.,* p. 164.

[11] *Izvestiia,* August 7 and 13, 1958.

[12] Kudriavtsev, *op. cit.*

[13] R. S. Livshits, *Ocherki po razmeshcheniiu promyshlennosti SSSR* (Essay on the Distribution of USSR Industry), Gospolitizdat, Moscow, 1954, pp. 16, 43.

[14] Miroshnikov and Zapolskii, *op. cit.*, p. 93.

[15] *Pravda*, November 19, 1957.

[16] *Ibid.*, January 14, 1960.

[17] *Ibid.*, January 15, 1960.

[18] *Ibid.*, October 25, 1959; *Izvestiia*, August 7, 1958.

[19] Gerhard H. E. Meissel, "Central Planning for Atomic Protection in the Eastern Bloc," *Wehrkunde*, 1959, No. 5.

[20] *Ibid.*

[21] Gvozdev and Iakovkin, *op. cit.*, p. 155.

[22] Miroshnikov and Zapolskii, *op. cit.*, pp. 92–93.

[23] *Ibid.*, p. 160.

[24] *Pravda*, May 12, 1959.

[25] Gvozdev and Iakovkin, *op. cit.*, p. 164.

[26] *Soviet News*, June 10, 1960.

[27] *Ibid.*

[28] Miroshnikov and Zapolskii, *op. cit.*, p. 93.

[29] Gvozdev and Iakovkin, *op. cit.*, p. 164.

[30] *Izvestiia*, August 7, 1958.

[31] *Soviet News*, June 10, 1960.

[32] P. A. Volodin *et al.*, *Novye raiony Moskvy* (New Districts of Moscow), Gosizdat literatury po stroitelstvu, arkhitekture i stroitelnym materialam, Moscow, 1960, *passim.*

[33] Maksimov, *op. cit.*, pp. 38–39; *Pravda*, August 19, 1960.

[34] *Pravda*, June 8, 1960.

CHAPTER 5

(Pp. 71–78)

[1] Ivanov, *op. cit.*, p. 37; *Umppt*, p. 13; Zubkin, *Individualnye sredstva*, p. 13.

[2] Miroshnikov and Zapolskii, *op. cit.*, p. 161.

[3] *Ibid.*; Zubkin, *Individualnye sredstva*, p. 13.

[4] Miroshnikov and Zapolskii, *op. cit.*, pp. 162–164.

[5] Moskalev *et al.*, *op. cit.*, pp. 91–92; Malshinskii, *op. cit.*, p. 37.

[6] Supron and Zverev, *op. cit.*, p. 294; Ivanov, *op. cit.*, p. 38; Zubkin, *Individualnye sredstva*, pp. 32–33.

[7] Zubkin, *Individualnye sredstva*, pp. 14–15; *MPVO v selskoi mestnosti*, p. 114.

[8] Miroshnikov and Zapolskii, *op. cit.*, pp. 176–179.

[9] *Ibid.*, pp. 180–184; Zubkin, *Individualnye sredstva*, pp. 33–34.

[10] V. M. Isachenko, *Zashchita selskokhoziaistvennykh zhivotnykh v usloviiakh napadeniia s vozdukha* (Protection of Farm Animals Under Condition of Attack from the Air), DOSAAF, Moscow, 1960, pp. 10–11.

[11] Miroshnikov and Zapolskii, *op. cit.*, p. 266; Gvozdev and Iakovkin, *op. cit.*, p. 183.

[12] Miroshnikov and Zapolskii, *op. cit.*, p. 178; Lebedeva, *op. cit.*, p. 22.

[13] Miroshnikov and Zapolskii, *op. cit.*, p. 184; Ivanov, *op. cit.*, pp. 52–53; *Umppt*, p. 29.

[14] *Umppt*, p. 29

[15] Miroshnikov and Zapolskii, *op. cit.*, p. 247; Zubkin, *Individualnye sredstva*, pp. 62–64; Lebedeva, *op. cit.*, pp. 27, 34.

[16] Miroshnikov and Zapolskii, *op. cit.*, p. 211; *Metodika podgotovki lichnogo sostava grupp samozashchity*, p. 46; G. Gromozdov, *Pervaia pomoshch postradavshemu v usloviiakh napadeniia s vozdukha* (First Aid to a Casualty Under Conditions of Attack from the Air), DOSAAF, Moscow, 1960, pp. 37–38; *Umppt*, pp. 74, 76.

[17] Miroshnikov and Zapolskii, *op. cit.*, p. 316.

[18] *MPVO v selskoi mestnosti*, p. 113.

[19] Popov and Reshetnikov, *op. cit.*, pp. 73–75.

[20] Arkhipov, *op. cit.*, p. 58; Moskalev *et al.*, *op. cit.*, pp. 101–103.

CHAPTER 6

(Pp. 79–110)

[1] *Umppt*, p. 32.

[2] Miroshnikov and Zapolskii, *op. cit.*, pp. 132–133; *MPVO v selskoi mestnosti*, p. 99.

[3] Doyle, *op. cit.*, p. A-1079.

[4] Supron and Zverev, *op. cit.*, p. 309.

[5] *Ibid.*, p. 308; Levin *et al.*, *op. cit.*, p. 91.

[6] Doyle, *op. cit.*, p. A-1079.

[7] Supron and Zverev, *op. cit.*, p. 308; Levin *et al.*, *op. cit.*, p. 95.

[8] Moskalev *et al.*, *op. cit.*, p. 63.

[9] Leon Gouré, "Soviet Civil Defense," in G. W. Baker and J. H. Rohrer (eds.), *Symposium on Human Problems in the Utilization of Fallout Shelters*, Disaster Study No. 12, Disaster Research Group, National Academy of Sciences—National Research Council, Washington, D.C., 1960, p. 105; Miroshnikov and Zapolskii, *op. cit.*, p. 133.

[10] Miroshnikov and Zapolskii, *op. cit.*, p. 113.

[11] Miroshnikov, *op. cit.*, p. 22; Gouré, *Symposium*, p. 105.

[12] Supron and Zverev, *op. cit.*, p. 307; Miroshnikov, *op. cit.*, p. 23; Moskalev *et al.*, *op. cit.*, p. 65.

[13] Doyle, *op. cit.*, p. A-1079; Gouré, *Symposium*, p. 105.

[14] Miroshnikov and Zapolskii, *op. cit.*, p. 134; Gouré, *Symposium*, p. 122; Supron and Zverev, *op. cit.*, p. 307.

[15] Gvozdev and Iakovkin, *op. cit.*, p. 173; Ivanov, *op. cit.*, p. 54; Lebedeva, *op. cit.*, pp. 7, 17; Diafilm, *Kollektivnye sredstva protivoatomnoi zashchity* (Collective Means of Anti-Atomic Defense), Moscow, 1958; *Umppt*, p. 32.

[16] *The Times-Picayune*, August 13, 1959; *Los Angeles Times*, July 26, 1959.

[17] Gvozdev and Iakovkin, *op. cit.*, p. 173.

[18] Fifth Report by the Committee on Government Operations, *op. cit.*, p. 93; *Pravda*, November 28, 1959

[19] *Moscow News*, March 14, 1959; *Pravda*, November 28, 1959.

[20] Fifth Report by the Committee on Government Operations, *op. cit.*, p. 94.

[21] Lebedeva, *op. cit.*, pp. 7 and 17.

[22] Fifth Report by the Committee on Government Operations, *op. cit.*, p. 94.

[23] *The New York Times*, September 30, 1954.

[24] Schellhammer, *op. cit.*, p. 145.

[25] Fifth Report by the Committee on Government Operations, *op. cit.*, p. 95.

[26] *Soviet News*, August 18, 1959.

[27] Leon Gouré, *Civil Defense 1961*, Hearings before a Subcommittee of the Committee on Government Operations, House of Representatives, Eighty-seventh Congress, First Session (U. S. Government Printing Office, Washington, D.C., 1961), p. 277.

[28] *Voennye znaniia*, 1957, No. 1, p. 24.

[29] Miroshnikov and Zapolskii, *op. cit.*, pp. 134–135.

[30] *Ibid.*, p. 139; Baratov, *op. cit.*, p. 134; Gvozdev and Iakovkin, *op. cit.*, p. 173.

[31] *Voennye znaniia*, 1957, No. 1, p. 24; Miroshnikov and Zapolskii, *op. cit.*, p. 135; Supron and Zverev, *op. cit.*, p. 306.

[32] Miroshnikov and Zapolskii, *op. cit.*, p. 136.

[33] Gouré, *Symposium*, p. 108.

[34] *Ibid.*; Doyle, *op. cit.*, p. A-1079.

[35] *Voennye znaniia*, 1957, No. 1, pp. 24–25; Supron and Zverev, *op. cit.*, p. 303; Lebedeva, *op. cit.*, p. 18; I. A. Koniushenko and A. M. Miasnenko (eds.), *Bakteriologicheskoe oruzhie i mery zaschity ot nego* (Bacteriological Weapons and Means of Defense Against Them), DOSAAF, Moscow, 1959, p. 7.

[36] Supron and Zverev, *op. cit.*, p. 304; Miroshnikov and Zapolskii, *op. cit.*, p. 140; Miroshnikov, *op. cit.*, p. 24.

[37] Lebedeva, *op. cit.*, p. 18; Miroshnikov, *op. cit.*, pp. 21–22; Arkhipov, *op. cit.*, p. 61; Kipriian, *op. cit.*, p. 55.

[38] Miroshnikov and Zapolskii, *op. cit.*, p. 137; *Voennye znaniia*, 1957, No. 1, p. 24.

[39] Gvozdev and Iakovkin, *op. cit.*, pp. 170–171; Miroshnikov and Zapolskii, *op. cit.*, p. 143; *Umppt*, p. 33; Miroshnikov, *op. cit.*, p. 26.

[40] *Voennye znaniia*, 1958, No. 9, p. 29.

[41] Supron and Zverev, *op. cit.*, p. 313; Miroshnikov and Zapolskii, *op. cit.*, p. 136; Moskalev *et al.*, *op. cit.*, p. 65.

[42] Supron and Zverev, *op. cit.*, p. 313.

[43] *Voennye znaniia,* 1958, No. 11, pp. 26–27.

[44] *Ibid.;* Miroshnikov and Zapolskii, *op. cit.*, pp. 143–144.

[45] *MPVO v selskoi mestnosti,* pp. 99–112.

[46] Supron and Zverev, *op. cit.*, p. 311; Miroshnikov and Zapolskii, *op. cit.*, pp. 146–155; Miroshnikov, *op. cit.*, p. 31.

[47] Miroshnikov and Zapolskii, *op. cit.*, pp. 150–151.

[48] Supron and Zverev, *op. cit.*, p. 309.

[49] *Ibid.*, p. 312; *Voennye znaniia,* 1957, No. 1, p. 25.

[50] Supron and Zverev, *op. cit.*, p. 312; Miroshnikov, *op. cit.*, pp. 31–32.

[51] *Voennye znaniia,* 1957, No. 1, p. 25.

[52] *Ibid.;* Supron and Zverev, *op. cit.*, p. 310; Miroshnikov and Zapolskii, *op. cit.*, pp. 144–149; Lebedeva, *op. cit.*, p. 19.

[53] Supron and Zverev, *op. cit.*, p. 310; Miroshnikov and Zapolskii, *op. cit.*, pp. 144–149; Lebedeva, *op. cit.*, p. 19.

[54] Miroshnikov and Zapolskii, *op. cit.*, p. 144; Supron and Zverev, *op. cit.*, p. 312; *Voennye znaniia,* 1957, No. 1, p. 25.

[55] *Sovetskii patriot,* July 1, 1959.

[56] Supron and Zverev, *op. cit.*, p. 312; *Voennye znaniia,* 1957, No. 3, p. 39.

[57] Kirillov, *op. cit.*, p. 53.

[58] Isachenko, *op. cit.*, p. 12.

[59] *MPVO v selskoi mestnosti,* p. 112.

[60] Volodin *et al.*, *op. cit.*, pp. 257–267.

[61] Supron and Zverev, *op. cit.*, p. 312.

[62] *Ibid.*, p. 113; Moskalev *et al.*, *op. cit.*, p. 73; Lebedeva, *op. cit.*, p. 17.

[63] Lebedeva, *op. cit.*, p. 17.

[64] *Ibid.*, p. 18; *Voennye znaniia,* 1959, No. 6, p. 25; Supron and Zverev, *op. cit.*, p. 304; Miroshnikov and Zapolskii, *op. cit.*, p. 140.

[65] Supron and Zverev, *op. cit.*, p. 305; *Voennye znaniia,* 1957, No. 1, p. 24.

[66] *Voennye znaniia,* 1959, No. 6, p. 25; 1957, No. 1, p. 24.

[67] Supron and Zverev, *op. cit.*, pp. 304–305; Miroshnikov and Zapolskii, *op. cit.*, pp. 140–141.

[68] *Voennye znaniia,* 1959, No. 6, p. 25.

[69] Diafilm, *Kollektivnye sredstva;* Levin *et al.*, *op. cit.*, p. 97; Moskalev *et al.*, *op. cit.*, p. 69.

[70] Miroshnikov and Zapolskii, *op. cit.*, p. 141; Gvozdev and Iakovkin, *op. cit.*, p. 164; Malshinskii, *op. cit.*, p. 59.

[71] Miroshnikov and Zapolskii, *op. cit.*, p. 266; Levin *et al.*, *op. cit.*, p. 112; Gvozdev and Iakovkin, *op. cit.*, p. 184; *Umppt,* p. 56.

[72] Lebedeva, *op. cit.*, p. 23.

[73] Miroshnikov and Zapolskii, *op. cit.*, p. 143; Levin *et al.*, *op. cit.*, p. 98; Gvozdev and Iakovkin, *op. cit.*, p. 170.

[74] Supron and Zverev, *op. cit.*, p. 98; Lebedeva and Serebriakov, *op. cit.*, p. 55; *Umppt,* p. 33.

[75] Miroshnikov and Zapolskii, *op. cit.*, p. 266; Levin *et al.*, *op. cit.*, p. 112; Gvozdev and Iakovkin, *op. cit.*, p. 184.
[76] Korablev, *op. cit.*, p. 3; Gorbunov *et al.*, *op. cit.*, pp. 15–16; Miroshnikov and Zapolskii, *op. cit.*, pp. 274–275.
[77] *Umppt*, p. 36.
[78] *Ibid.*, p. 38; Miroshnikov and Zapolskii, *op. cit.*, p. 269.
[79] *Voennye znaniia*, 1960, No. 10, p. 32.
[80] Diafilm, *Kollektivnye sredstva;* Miroshnikov and Zapolskii, *op. cit.*, pp. 159–160.
[81] Miroshnikov and Zapolskii, *op. cit.*, pp. 159–160.
[82] *Bulletin of the Atomic Scientists*, May, 1959.
[83] *Umppt*, pp. 36–37.
[84] *Ibid.*, p. 35.
[85] Supron and Zverev, *op. cit.*, p. 309; *Magyar Legoltalom* (Hungarian Civil Defense), October, 1960.
[86] Fifth Report by the Committee on Government Operations, *op. cit.*, p. 63.
[87] *Ibid.*
[88] *Ibid.*, p. 64.
[89] *Ibid.*
[90] Miroshnikov and Zapolskii, *op. cit.*, pp. 91–93; Gvozdev and Iakovkin, *op. cit.*, pp. 155 and 164.
[91] *Umppt*, pp. 31–38; *Umpppv*, pp. 41–52; *Voennye znaniia*, 1959, No. 4, pp. 34–35.
[92] *Sovetskii patriot*, May 20 and July 1, 1959; February 17, 1960; February 19, 1961.
[93] *Ibid.*, May 20, 1959.
[94] *Ibid.*, January 16, 1960; September 3, 1961.
[95] *Ibid.*, August 11, December 15, 1957; June 11, August 6, 1958; May 20, July 1, 1959; February 10 and 17, March 13, 1960; February 12 and 19, September 13, 1961; *Voennye znaniia*, 1957, No. 12, p. 33; 1959, No. 3, p. 32.
[96] *The New York Times*, May 17, 1961.

CHAPTER 7

(Pp. 111–118)

[1] Gvozdev and Iakovkin, *op. cit.*, p. 159.
[2] *Ibid.*, p. 236.
[3] Miroshnikov and Zapolskii, *op. cit.*, p. 82.
[4] *Ibid.*, p. 84.
[5] *Voennye znaniia*, 1958, No. 9, p. 30.
[6] *Sovetskii patriot*, October 8, 1958.
[7] *Umpppv*, pp. 24–26.
[8] *Voennye znaniia*, 1960, No. 7, pp. 33–34.

[9] *Ibid.*, p. 33; Korablev, *op. cit.*, p. 7; *Umpppv*, pp. 25–26.
[10] Miroshnikov and Zapolskii, *op. cit.*, p. 89; *Voennye znaniia*, 1960, No. 7, p. 33.
[11] *Voennye znaniia*, 1960, No. 7, p. 34; *Umpppv*, p. 25.
[12] *Voennye znaniia*, 1960, No. 7, p. 34.
[13] *Ibid.*, p. 33.
[14] *Ibid.*, p. 34.
[15] *Ibid.*; Korablev, *op. cit.*, p. 7; Leon Gouré, *Civil Defense 1961*, p. 290.
[16] *Umpppv*, p. 25; *Voennye znaniia*, 1960, No. 7, p. 34.
[17] *Umpppv*, p. 26; *Voennye znaniia*, 1960, No. 7, p. 34.
[18] *Umpppv*, p. 26.
[19] *Voennye znaniia*, 1960, No. 7, p. 34.
[20] *Ibid.*, p. 33.
[21] *Ibid.*, p. 34.
[22] *Voennye znaniia*, 1960, No. 10, p. 32.
[23] *Ibid.*, 1959, No. 6, p. 23.
[24] *Ibid.*, 1957, No. 2, p. 22; 1959, No. 1, p. 28; 1960, No. 10, p. 32; *Umpppv*, pp. 33–34; Gvozdev and Iakovkin, *op. cit.*, pp. 219–220.
[25] *Umpppv*, p. 34; Gvozdev and Iakovkin, *op. cit.*, p. 220.
[26] Gvozdev and Iakovkin, *op. cit.*, p. 220; Miroshnikov and Zapolskii, *op. cit.*, pp. 269–271; *Voennye znaniia*, 1960, No. 10, p. 33.
[27] Dinerstein and Gouré, *op. cit.*, pp. 182–183.
[28] Fifth Report by the Committee on Government Operations, *op. cit.*, p. 95.
[29] *Soviet News*, February 2, 1961; N. S. Kruschev, "Control Figures," in *Decisions of the Twenty-First Extraordinary Congress of the Communist Party of the Soviet Union, January 27–February 5, 1959*, Foreign Languages Publishing House, Moscow, 1959, p. 101.
[30] Karasev, *op. cit.*, p. 200.
[31] Dinerstein and Gouré, *op. cit.*, pp. 200–201.

CHAPTER 8

(Pp. 119–138)

[1] Miroshnikov and Zapolskii, *op. cit.*, p. 89.
[2] *Ibid.*, pp. 91–112; Gvozdev and Iakovkin, *op. cit.*, p. 156; *Umpppv*, pp. 52–54; *MPVO v selskoi mestnosti*, pp. 79–98.
[3] Colonel N. P. Iakovlev *et al.*, *Uchebnik doprizyvnika* (Manual for Pre-Conscription Youth), Voenizdat Ministerstva Oborony Soiuza SSR, Moscow, 1960, p. 81.
[4] *Umppt*, p. 55.
[5] Miroshnikov and Zapolskii, *op. cit.*, p. 267; Korablev, *op. cit.*, pp. 9–10.
[6] *Ibid.*; Gvozdev and Iakovkin, *op. cit.*, p. 184.
[7] *Umpppv*, p. 55.
[8] *Ibid.*, pp. 57–58; Miroshnikov and Zapolskii, *op. cit.*, pp. 90–91.

[9] Tsentralnoe Statisticheskoe Upravlenie pri Sovete Ministrov SSSR (Central Statistical Directory of the Soviet of Ministers of the USSR), *Narodnoe Khoziaistvo SSSR v 1958 godu, statisticheskii ezhegodnik* (The National Economy of the USSR in 1958, Statistical Yearbook), Gosizdat, Moscow, 1959, p. 602.

[10] N. S. Khrushchev, "Control Figures," in *Decisions of the Twenty-First Extraordinary Congress of the Communist Party of the Soviet Union, January 27–February 5, 1959,* Foreign Languages Publishing House, Moscow, 1959, p. 102.

[11] Miroshnikov and Zapolskii, *op. cit.*, p. 188.

[12] *Ibid.*, p. 121.

[13] *Ibid.*

[14] *Ibid.*, pp. 85–86, 122–123; Korablev, *op. cit.*, p. 6.

[15] Miroshnikov and Zapolskii, *op. cit.*, pp. 94–97.

[16] *Ibid.*, p. 97.

[17] *Voennye znaniia,* 1958, No. 9, p. 30; *MPVO v selskoi mestnosti,* pp. 75–81.

[18] *Voennye znaniia,* 1957, No. 3, pp. 23–24; 1958, No. 9, p. 30; 1959, No. 1, pp. 28–29; Lebedeva, *op. cit.*, pp. 103–107; Miroshnikov and Zapolskii, *op. cit.*, pp. 103–107.

[19] *The New York Times,* January 22 and February 3, 1960.

[20] Miroshnikov and Zapolskii, *op. cit.*, pp. 103–105; Lebedeva, *op. cit.*, p. 23.

[21] *MPVO v selskoi mestnosti,* pp. 81–98; Lebedeva, *op. cit.*, p. 23; Miroshnikov and Zapolskii, *op. cit.*, pp. 103–120.

[22] Isachenko, *op. cit.*, pp. 32–34; *MPVO v selskoi mestnosti,* pp. 85–90; V. R. Borodin, *Zashchita selskokhoziaistvennykh zhivotnykh ot bakteriologicheskogo oruzhiia* (Protection of Farm Animals Against Bacteriological Weapons), Ministerstvo Selskogo Khoziaistva Turkmenskoi SSR, Ashkhabad, 1960, pp. 19–23.

[23] Supron and Zverev, *op. cit.*, p. 19.

[24] *Umpppv,* p. 3.

[25] Supron and Zverev, *op. cit.*, p. 20; *Umpppv,* p. 4.

[26] Supron and Zverev, *op. cit.*, pp. 251, 274–276; Levin *et al.*, *op. cit.*, p. 116; Miroshnikov and Zapolskii, *op. cit.*, p. 248; Gvozdev and Iakovkin, *op. cit.*, p. 237.

[27] Miroshnikov and Zapolskii, *op. cit.*, p. 187; Supron and Zverev, *op. cit.*, p. 162.

[28] Gromozdov, *op. cit., passim;* Supron and Zverev, *op. cit., passim; Voennye znaniia,* 1961, No. 3, pp. 32–33.

[29] Supron and Zverev, *op. cit.*, p. 287.

[30] *Ibid.*, p. 274.

[31] *Ibid.*, pp. 255–591.

[32] *Ibid.*, pp. 152–166; V. S. Balabukha (ed.), *Khimicheskaia zashchita organizma ot ioniziruiushchikh izluchenii* (Chemical Protection of the Organism Against Ionizing Radiation), Izdatelstvo Glavnovo Upravleniia po

Izpolzovaniiu Atomnoi Energii pri Sovete Ministrov SSSR, Moscow, 1960. *passim;* D. I. Zakutinskii and L. N. Selivanova, *Biologicheskaia otsenka preparator dlia profiliaktiki i lechenii luchevoi bolezni* (Biological Evaluation of Compounds for Prophylactic and Treatment of Radiation Sickness), Medgiz, Moscow, 1960, *passim; Los Angeles Times,* November 8, 1961.

[33] *Pravda,* January 20, 1960.

[34] Miroshnikov and Zapolskii, *op. cit.,* p. 42.

[35] *Voennye znaniia,* 1959, No. 8, pp. 32–33.

[36] G. Makushenko and I. Novichenko, *Zazhigatelyne sredstva i protivopozharnaia zashchita* (Incendiary Agents and Anti-Fire Defense), DOSAAF, Moscow, 1958, p. 23.

[37] Miroshnikov and Zapolskii, *op. cit.,* p. 224; Makushenko and Novichenko, *op. cit.,* pp. 28–45; G. T. Makushenko, *Deistviia zvena protivopozharnoi zashchity mestnoi PVO* (Actions of the Fire-Fighting Team of the Local Anti-Air Defense), DOSAAF, 1960, pp. 5–50; *Voennye znaniia,* 1961, No. 2, pp. 34–35.

[38] Neiman and Sadilenko, *op. cit.,* pp. 120–127; Levin *et al., op. cit.,* p. 41; N. P. Petrov, *Radioaktivnye izlucheniia i ikh izmereniia* (Radioactive Emissions and Their Measurement), Voenizdat, Moscow, 1956, p. 111; Zubkin, *Chto takoe,* p. 10; Supron and Zverev, *op. cit.,* pp. 95, 108; A. I. Ivanov and G. I. Rybkin, *Porazhaiushchee deistvie iadernogo vzryva* (The Damaging Effect of a Nuclear Explosion), Voenizdat Ministerstva Oborony Soiuza SSR, Moscow, 1960, p. 329; Miroshnikov and Zapolskii, *op. cit.,* p. 270; *Voennye znaniia,* 1956, No. 6, p. 17.

[39] Gvozdev and Iakovkin, *op. cit.,* p. 221.

[40] Zubkin, *Chto takoe,* pp. 10–11.

[41] Miroshnikov and Zapolskii, *op. cit.,* pp. 237–238.

[42] Levin *et al., op. cit.,* pp. 124–132; Supron and Zverev, *op. cit.,* pp. 337–385; K. S. Kalugin *et al., Prakticheskoe rukovodstvo po dozimetrii* (Practical Instructions on Dose Metering), Medgiz, Moscow, 1959, pp. 29–85.

[43] Miroshnikov and Zapolskii, *op. cit.,* pp. 238–239; *Voennye znaniia,* 1961, No. 1, p. 31; Baratov, *op. cit.,* p. 167.

[44] Miroshnikov and Zapolskii, *op. cit.,* p. 316; *Voennye znaniia,* 1958, No. 11, p. 24.

[45] Miroshnikov and Zapolskii, *op. cit.,* p. 270; Levin *et al., op. cit.,* p. 113.

[46] Supron and Zverev, *op. cit.,* pp. 389–392; Lebedeva, *op. cit.,* p. 32; Zubkin, *Individualnye sredstva,* pp. 60–61; Gvozdev and Iakovkin, *op. cit.,* pp. 233–234; *Voennye znaniia,* 1960, No. 10, p. 33.

[47] Miroshnikov and Zapolskii, *op. cit.,* pp. 244–248; Gvozdev and Iakovkin, *op. cit.,* pp. 222–235; Levin *et al., op. cit.,* pp. 152–153; Zubkin, *Chto takoe,* pp. 11–20; Stavrov, *op. cit.,* pp. 50–61; *Voennye znaniia,* 1960, No. 10, pp. 32–33.

[48] Lebedeva, *op. cit.,* pp. 32–39; *Voennye znaniia,* 1960, No. 7, p. 34; No. 10, pp. 32–33.

[49] *Voennye znaniia,* 1959, No. 1, p. 29; No. 2, p. 29; Lebedeva and Serebriakov, *op. cit.,* pp. 92–108; Miroshnikov and Zapolskii, *op. cit.,* pp. 253–264.

[50] Isachenko, *op. cit.*, pp. 34–63; Borodin, *op. cit.*, pp. 23–30; *MPVO v selskoi mestnosti*, pp. 165–189; *Voennye znaniia*, 1959, No. 1, pp. 27–28; No. 6, pp. 23–24.

[51] *Voennye znaniia*, 1956, No. 6, p. 15; Lebedeva, *op. cit.*, pp. 38–39; Supron and Zverev, *op. cit.*, pp. 385–399, 402–404; Miroshnikov and Zapolskii, *op. cit.*, p. 264; Zubkin, *Chto takoe*, pp. 44–55.

CHAPTER 9

(Pp. 139–151)

[1] *Pravda*, June 1, 1959.

[2] *Ibid.*, July 30, 1959.

[3] *Ibid.*, January 15, 1960. For a discussion of Soviet views on deterrence and surprise attack, see A. L. Horelick, "'Deterrence' and Surprise in Soviet Strategic Thought," *R.C.A.F. Staff College Journal*, 1960.

[4] *Pravda*, October 25, 1961.

[5] Janos Dobra, "Civil Defense for the Rural Population," *Bekes Megyei Nepujsag*, August 2, 1961, as quoted in *Current* (New York), October, 1961, p. 39.

BIBLIOGRAPHY

BOOKS AND PAMPHLETS

Arkhipov, M. P. *Osnovy ustroistva atomnogo oruzhiia i protivoatomnaia zashchita.* Moscow: DOSAAF, 1956.

Bakteriologicheskoe oruzhie i mery zashchity ot nego, eds. Ia. Koniushenko and A. M. Miashnenko. Moscow: DOSAAF, 1959.

Baratov, G. F. *Mestnaia protivovozdushnaia oborona naseleniia v usloviiakh khimicheskogo, atomnogo i bakteriologicheskogo napadeniia.* Kiev: Gosizdat Meditsinskoe Izdatelstvo SSSR, 1959.

Bibergal, A. V., and U. Ia Margulis. *Atomnyi vzryv i nekotorye voprosy protivoatomnoi zashchity.* Moscow: Medgiz, 1958.

Bolshaia sovetskaia entsiklopediia, vol. 40, 2d ed.; Moscow: Gosudarstvennoe nauchnoe izdatelstvo "Bolshaia sovetskaia entsiklopediia," 1957.

Borodin, V. R. *Zashchita selskokhoziaistvennykh zhivotnykh ot bakteriologicheskogo oruzhiia.* Ashkabad: Ministerstvo selskogo khoziaistva Turkmenskoi SSR, 1960.

Decisions of the Twenty-First Extraordinary Congress of the Communist Party of the Soviet Union, January 27–February 5, 1959. Moscow: Foreign Languages Publishing House, 1959.

Dinerstein, H. S. *War and the Soviet Union.* New York: Praeger, 1959.

Dinerstein, H. S., and Leon Gouré. *Two Studies in Soviet Controls.* Glencoe, Illinois: Free Press, 1955.

Dolbnin, T. V. *Bakteriologicheskogo oruzhie i mery zashchity ot nego.* Moscow: DOSAAF, 1959.

Doyle, Hon. Clyde. *Appendix, Congressional Record,* February 20, 1961.

Fifth Report by the Committee on Government Operations, "Civil Defense in Western Europe and the Soviet Union," House Report No. 300. Washington, D.C.: U.S. Government Printing Office, 1959.

Garthoff, R. L. *Soviet Military Doctrine.* Glencoe, Ill.: Free Press, 1953.

———. *Soviet Strategy in the Nuclear Age.* New York: Praeger, 1959.

Gorbunov, I., K. Kotlunov, and V. Moskalev. *Deistviia grupp samozashchity i ikh podgotovka.* Moscow: DOSAAF, 1957.

Gouré, Leon. *Soviet Civil Defense.* The Rand Corporation, P-1887. Revised March 14, 1960. [Condensed version in *Air Force and Space* Digest, August, 1961, pp. 38–41.]

———, "Soviet Civil Defense," in *Symposium on Human Problems in the Utilization of Fallout Shelters,* eds. G. W. Baker and J. H. Rohrer. Washington, D.C.: National Academy of Sciences, National Research Council, 1960.

———, *Civil Defense 1961,* Hearings before a Subcommittee of the Committee on Government Operations, House of Representatives, Eighty-seventh Congress, First Session, August 1–8, 9, 1961. Washington, D.C.: U.S. Government Printing Office. Pp. 263–303.

Gromozdov, G. *Pervaia pomoshch postradavshemu v usloviiakh napadeniia s vozdukha.* Moscow: DOSAAF, 1960.

Gvozdev, M., and V. Iakovkin. *Atomnoe oruzhie i protivoatomnaia zashchita.* 2d ed.; Moscow: DOSAAF, 1958.

Iakovlev, Col. N. P., Col. N. A. Sokolov, Lt. Col. N. A. Beshkarev, and P. V. Fediaev. *Uchebnik doprizyvnika.* Moscow: Voenizdat Ministerstva Oborony Soiuza SSR, 1960.

Independent Offices Appropriations for 1962, Hearings before the Subcommittee of the Committee on Appropriations, House of Representatives, Eighty-seventh Congress, First Session. Washington, D.C.: U.S. Government Printing Office, 1961.

Isachenko, V. M. *Zashchita selskokhoziaistvennykh zhivotnykh v usloviiakh napadeniia s vozdukha.* Moscow: DOSAAF, 1960.

Ivanov, N. *Bud gotov k PVO.* Moscow: DOSAAF, 1959.

Ivanov, A. I., and G. I. Rybkin. *Porazhaiushchee deistvie iadernogo vzryva.* Moscow: Voenizdat Ministerstva Oborony Soiuza SSR, 1960.

Kalugin, K. S., U. Ia Margulis, K. A. Trukhanov, and L. S. Uspenskii. *Prakticheskoe rukovodstvo po dozimetrii.* Moscow: Medgiz, 1959.

Karasev, A. V. *Leningradtsy v gody blokady.* Moscow: Akademii Nauk SSSR, 1959.

Khimicheskaia zashchita organizma ot ioniziruiushchikh izluchenii, ed. V. S. Balabukha. Moscow: Izdatelstvo Glavnogo Upravleniia po Izpolzovaniiu Atomnoi Energii pri Sovete Ministrov SSSR, 1960.

Kipriian, K. *Kak organizovat priem norm "Gotov k PVO" vtoroi stupeni.* Moscow: DOSAAF, 1960.

Kirillov, P. M. *Dosaafovtsu o MPVO.* Moscow: DOSAAF, 1956.

Komsomol i DOSAAF. *Molodaia gvardia.* Moscow: 1954.

Korablev, M. D. *Okhrana obshchestvennogo poriadka i bezopasnosti v usloviiakh PVO.* Moscow: DOSAAF, 1960.

Korablev, M. D., Iu. Lebedeva, and L. Shesterikova. *MPVO v selskoi mestnosti.* Moscow: DOSAAF, 1959.

Kozlova, A. V. *Posledstviia vzryvov atomnykh bomb v Khirosima i Nagasaki i vodorodnoi bomby v Bikini.* Moscow: Medgiz, 1957.

Kudriavtsev, A. "Care of Man is the Basis of Soviet City Planning," Press Department release, No. 353, Embassy of the USSR, Washington, D.C., July 21, 1960.

Lebedeva, Iu., and V. Serebriakov. *Bakteriologicheskoe oruzhie innostrannykh armii i zashchita ot nego.* Moscow: DOSAAF, 1957.

Lenin, V. I., "Report of the Central Committee at the 8th Party Congress," in his *Selected Works,* Vol. VIII. New York: International Publishing House, 1943.

Levin, M. E., G. A. Malinin, M. N. Mandrazhitskii, V. P. Sinitsyn, and V. F. Fedorov. *Zashchita ot sredstv massovogo porazheniia.* Moscow: Gosudarstvennoe uchebno-pedagogicheskoe izdatelstvo Ministerstva Proveshcheniia RSFSR, 1958.

Livshits, R. S. *Ocherki po razmeshcheniiu promyshlennosti* SSSR. Moscow: Gospolitizdat, 1954.

Makushenko, G. T. *Deistviia zvena protivopozharnoi zashchity mestnoi PVO.* Moscow: DOSAAF, 1960.

Makushenko, G. T., and I. Novichenko. *Zazhigatelnye sredstva i protivopozharnaia zashchita.* Moscow: DOSAAF, 1958.

Malshinskii, A. *Khimicheskoe oruzhie innostrannykh armii i protivokhimicheskaia zashchita.* Moscow: DOSAAF, 1957.

Meisel, J. H., and E. S. Kozera. *Materials for the Study of the Soviet System.* Ann Arbor, Mich.: George Wahr, 1950.

Metodika podgotovki lichnogo sostava grupp samozashchity. Moscow: DOSAAF, 1959.

Miroshnikov, I. P. *Kollektivnye sredstva protivoatomnoi zashchity.* Moscow: DOSAAF, 1951.

Miroshnikov, I. P., and G. N. Zapolskii, eds. *Zashchita naseleniia ot sovremennykh sredstv porazheniia.* Moscow: DOSAAF, 1959.

Moskalev, V. D., V. P. Sinitsyn, and A. S. Tertychnyi, eds. *Uchebnoe posobie po MPVO.* Moscow: DOSAAF, 1956, 1957.

Narodnoe khoziaistvo SSSR v 1958 gode, statisticheskii ezhegodnik, Tsentralnoe statisticheskoe upravlenie pri Sovete Ministrov SSSR. Moscow: Gosizdat, 1959.

Neiman, M. V., and K. M. Sadilenko. *Termoiadernoe oruzhie.* Moscow: Voenizdat Ministerstva Oborony Soiuza SSR, 1959.

Pamiatka naseleniiu po zashchite ot atomnogo, khimicheskogo i bakteriologicheskogo oruzhiia. Moscow: DOSAAF, 1957.

Pamiatka naseleniiu po zashchite ot atomnogo oruzhiia. Moscow: DOSAAF, 1954.

Petrov, N. P. *Radioaktivnye izlucheniia i ikh izmereniia.* Moscow: Voenizdat, 1956.

Pokrovskii, Maj. Gen. G. I. *Rol nauki i tekhniki v sovremennoi voine.* Moscow: "Znanie," 1957.

———. *Science and Technology in Contemporary War.* New York: Praeger, 1959.

Popov, G. M., and P. P. Reshetnikov. *Kratkie osnovy meditsinskoi sluzhby mestnoi protivovozdushnoi oborony dlia srednego meditsinskogo personala.* Moscow: Medgiz, 1951.

Savitskii, I. I. *MPVO zhilogo doma.* Moscow: DOSAAF, 1951.

Savitskii, I. I., and P. M. Kirillov. *Protipovitriana oborona.* Kiev: DTVU, 1953.

Sputnik komsomolskogo aktivista. Moscow: Molodaia gvardiia, 1960.

Sredstva i sposoby protivovozdushnoi oborony naseleniia. Moscow: DOSAAF, 1958.

Standard Metropolitan Statistical Areas, Executive Office of the President, Bureau of the Budget. Washington, D.C.: U.S. Government Printing Office, 1961.

Stavrov, B. *Rabota voditelia avtomobilia v usloviiakh primeneniia atomnogo, khimicheskogo i bakteriologicheskogo oruzhiia.* Moscow: DOSAAF, 1960.

Stolpner, B. *Prevratim Leningrad v nepristupnuiu krepost oborony.* Leningrad: Gazetno-zhurnalnoe i knizhnoe izdatelstvo Leningradskogo Soveta RKIKD, 1939.

Supron, L. F., and F. P. Zverev. *Meditsinskoe obespechenie naseleniia v usloviiakh primeneniia sredstv massovogo porazheniia.* Minsk: Gosizdat, BSSR, 1959.

Uchebno-metodicheskoe posobie po prakticheskoe podgotovke vzroslogo naseleniia k deistviiam po likvidatsii posledstvii napadeniia s vozdukha. Moscow: DOSAAF, 1960.

Uchebno-metodicheskoe posobie po provedeniiu trenirovok i priemu norm "Gotov k PVO" 1-i stupeni. Moscow: DOSAAF, 1959.

Volin, S., and R. M. Slusser, eds. *The Soviet Secret Police.* New York: Praeger, 1957.

Volodin, P. A., A. M. Zhuravlev, *et al. Novye raiony Moskvy.* Moscow: Gosizdat literatury po stroitelstvy arkhitekture i stroitelnym materialam, 1960.

Werth, A. *Moscow War Diary.* New York: Knopf, 1942.

Zakutinskii, D. I., and L. N. Selivanova. *Biologicheskaia otsenka preparatov dlia profilaktiki i lecheniia luchevoi bolezni.* Moscow: Medgiz, 1960.

Zubkin, A. S. *Individualnye sredstva protivokhimicheskoe zashchity.* Moscow: DOSAAF, 1958.

———. *Chto takoe dezaktivatsiia i degazatsiia.* Moscow: DOSAAF, 1960.

JOURNALS

Aksim, Maj. R. E., CD, "Survival Operations in the USSR," *Canadian Army Journal,* No. 2, 1960.

Baz, Col. I. S., "Soviet Military Science on the Character of Contemporary War," *Voennyi vestnik,* No. 6, 1958.

Bulletin of the Atomic Scientists, May, 1959.

Dubinin, M., and A. Imshenetsky, "The Danger of Biological and Chemical Weapons," *International Affairs,* No. 11, 1959.

Horelick, A. L., "'Deterrence' and Surprise in Soviet Strategic Thought," *R.C.A.F. Staff College Journal,* 1960.

Imshenetsky, A., "Microbiology Must Not Serve Death," *Mezhdunarodnaia zhizn,* No. 2, 1961.

Kapitsa, P., "The Task of the Entire Progressive Mankind," *Novoe vremiia,* No. 39, 1956.

Khodjaiev, D., "Villes de Demain," *Études Soviétiques,* No. 156, March, 1961.

Kravtsov, Col. I. V., "The Role of the Air Force in the Aggressive Plans of N.A.T.O.," *Vestnik vozdushnogo flota,* No. 12, 1957.

Magyar Kozloni, No. 112, December 18, 1960.

Magyar Legoltalom, October, 1960.

Maksimov, G. M., "Movement and Composition of the Population of the USSR," *Istoriia SSSR,* No. 1, 1961.

Meissel, Gerhard H. E., "Central Planning for Atomic Protection in the Eastern Bloc," *Wehrkunde,* No. 5, 1959.

Schellhammer, H., "Die Problematik des Luftschutzes in Atomzeitalter," *Wehrkunde,* No. 3, 1959.

Sovetskii krasnyi krest, Nos. 2 and 5, 1957.

"Soviet Civil Defense Against CBR Attack," *Armed Forces Chemical Journal,* No. 3, May–June, 1959.

Talenskii, Maj. Gen. N., "The Soviet Disarmament Program and Its Critics," *International Affairs,* No. 11, 1959.

———, "On the Character of Modern Warfare," *International Affairs,* No. 10, 1960.

Voennye znaniia, January, 1953–April, 1961.

Za oboronu, Nos. 1, 11, 12, 13/14, 23/24, 1946.

NEWSPAPERS

Bekes Megyei Nepujsag, August 2, 1961.

Izvestiia, March 15, 1939; August 7 and 13, 1958; May 10, 1959.

Krasnaia zvezda, January 23, September 26, 1957; January 10 and 18, 1961.
Leningradskaia pravda, July 29, 1941.
The Los Angeles Times, July 26, 1959; November 8, 1961.
Moscow News, March 14, 1959.
The New York Times, September 30, 1954; June 28, 1959; January 22, February 3, 1960; May 17, 1961.
Pravda, January, 1956–October, 1961.
Sovetskaia aviatsiia, August 12, 1958.
Sovetskii patriot, January, 1957–October, 1961.
Soviet News, August 18, 1959; June 9 and 10, 1960; February 2, 1961.
The Times-Picayune (New Orleans), August 13, 1959.

DIAFILM [*Film Strips*]

Kollektivnye sredstva protivoatomnoi zashchity. Moscow, 1956.

INDEX

Abbreviations

CD	Civil Defense
DOSAAF	*Dobrovolnoe obshchestvo sodeistviia armii, aviatsii i flotu*
MPVO	*Mestnaia Protivovozdushnaia Oborona*

Index

www.ingramcontent.com/pod-product-compliance
Lightning Source LLC
LaVergne TN
LVHW011512200926
848484LV00001B/20
* 9 7 8 0 3 1 3 2 5 1 6 2 7 *